50 GUNS
THAT CHANGED THE WORLD

50 GUNS
THAT CHANGED THE WORLD

ICONIC FIREARMS THAT
ALTERED THE COURSE OF HISTORY

ROBERT A. SADOWSKI

Skyhorse Publishing

Visit our website at www.skyhorsepublishing.com.

10 9 8 7 6 5 4 3 2 1

Library of Congress Cataloging-in-Publication Data is available on file.

Cover design by Richard Rossiter
Cover images courtesy of the author

Paperback ISBN: 978-1-5107-7265-6
Hardcover ISBN: 978-1-63450-445-4
Ebook ISBN: 978-1-63450-463-8

Printed in China

Table of Contents

Introduction

Picking the fifty best, most iconic firearms is no easy task. There were some obvious choices, like the Winchester Model 1873 lever-action rifle and the Mossberg 500 pump-action shotgun as well as the Ruger Mark I semiautomatic rimfire pistol—guns that have indelibly changed the way we hunt, shoot competitively, and defend ourselves. Other selections may send you into fits of fury or have you sit back in contentment. Including firearms that everyone could purchase and own—depending on the thickness of your wallet, or lack thereof—was important. Not all of these guns are favorites of mine, but they made the list due to what their design brought to the shooting community and their influence on future firearm designs. Pop culture has had an influence on guns, though notoriety is not a substitute for performance. Production runs are a good indicator of a firearm's popularity and durability, and I figured that into my highly unscientific equations. With no apologies, here are fifty guns that changed the world.

NINETEENTH CENTURY

Parker Brothers VH Grade

The Old Reliable
Produced: 1866–1934 (Remington 1934–1942)

The Parker brothers—Wilbur, Dexter, and Charles—were not that jazzed about their dad's early manufacturing business. Their father, Charles Parker, operated a small shop that manufactured a variety of goods such as coffee mills, doorknockers, waffle irons, door hinges, and numerous other items. The brothers were more interested in what dad started producing later on. Charles Parker was a crafty businessman and partnered with a number of other investors. At the beginning of the Civil War Parker and his partners won contracts from the Union Army to produce thousands of rifles. After the war Parker became the sole owner of the Meriden Manufacturing Company and the first shotguns produced with the Parker name were roll marked "Made by the Meriden Man'f Co. for Charles Parker" and are known as the T-latch or back-action guns, as well as Dollar Grade guns. At the time Parker did not have a grading system in place, so later collectors rated the guns on how many dollars a customer had to spend (which determined the level of embellishments). By the time his sons were working with him, Parker shotguns had established a name for quality, handcrafted work manufactured in Meriden, Connecticut. Czars, movie stars, leaders in industry, United States presidents, and generals owned Parker shotguns. The gilded age of side-by-side shotguns was from about 1888 through the 1930s, and Parker shotguns quickly made a name for themselves among the numerous American-made side-by-sides of the time. Gun manufacturing flourished in the Connecticut River Valley, similar to the role Silicon Valley played in computer and software development. Parkers, and all guns of this era, were hand-built from machined parts. Buyers could order a gun made to their specifications—gauge, barrel lengths, triggers, frame size, barrel rib, wood, and engraving were only limited by a customer's budget. Duck hunters to trapshooters to those upland hunters chasing grouse or coveys of quails, they all had a Parker made to order. To this day Parkers are coveted by collectors; many are not just kept in gun safes but are refurbished and used for clay shooting and hunting.

Side-by-side shotguns may seem as relevant in the twenty-first century as buggy whips, but these firearms played an important role in our western expansion after the Civil War as well as with hunters and sportsmen up until the 1930s. Back then the side-by-side shotgun was humble and could be had for a song—or a king's ransom. The side-by-side was in nearly every wagon hauling westward, and it was used to collect meat for the pot and protect the homestead. Other side-by-side manufacturers in Connecticut and elsewhere in the north were churning out shotguns, but none would be as mythical as Parker. As society had more free time and industry churned, men from places like New York City would board trains heading north to Connecticut, Rhode Island, and elsewhere in New England or out on Long Island for a little "gunning." With them was a leather-cased shotgun, and many times the gun was a Parker. The Parker was nicknamed "The Old Reliable."

The epitome of Parker craftsmanship was the Invincible. According to legend (many collectors speak of Parkers in reverent, almost mythical tones), the first Invincible was manufactured in 1923 and cost $1,250 back then. This rare 16-gauge gun was in a private collection and rarely photographed, but it has since been put on display at the National Rifle Association (NRA) museum. The Invincible has exquisite engraving with gold inlays of game birds on the side and bottom of the receiver. The wood is lavishly checkered. Two others are believed to exist today. As ostentatious as the Invincible is, the majority of Parkers were less garish. For the fifty years the Parker Brothers Company was in business, they produced about 243,000 shotguns in total. The most widely produced Parker was the VH grade, which featured a top latch. Parkers went through several design changes over the years. The VH was introduced with Vulcan steel barrels, some wood checkering, and a little engraving on the frame. All the metal work, save the barrels, was case-hardened. Later guns have a hard rubber butt plate molded with a dog's head.

Specifications

GAUGE: 10, 12, 16, 20, 28, .410

BARREL LENGTH: 26 inches to 32 inches

WEIGHT: 6.9 pounds to 8.5 pounds

STOCK: Select checkered walnut; straight, half-, or full-pistol grip

SIGHTS: Bead

ACTION: Boxlock, break-action

FINISH: Case-hardened frame/blued barrel

CAPACITY: 2

The Parker Reproduction

In a similar way that Colt SAA revolvers and Winchester 1873 rifles have been reproduced, the Parker was revived in the 1980s. By this time all quality American side-by-side shotgun makers—A.H. Fox, L.C. Smith, Parker, Winchester—were long out of business, but there was still a desire for a high quality side-by-side shotgun among collectors and shooters. The Parker seemed the natural choice to reproduce as the most aristocratic of the American breed. The "repro" Parkers were made in Japan by Olin Kodensha and are fine examples of the gunmaker's art. DHE, B, and A-1 grade models were made, many with two-barrel sets. Today, Connecticut Shotgun Manufacturing Company in New Britain, Connecticut, makes a reproduction of the Parker, the A.H. Fox, and the Winchester Model 21 and is the last of the great American side-by-side shotgun manufacturers.

Above: Remington Arms Company and Connecticut Shotgun Manufacturing Company build a reproduction of a Parker AAHE 28-gauge with a variety of options that starts at $49,000.

Left: An advertisement from the turn of the nineteenth century touting the Parker taking the first and second prizes at the Grand American competition.

Other Notable American Doubles

Want to ruffle feathers? Then leave out one of the fine American doubles from a list of iconic guns. There was the Parker, but there was also the A.H. Fox, which was manufactured from 1903–1946. Today Connecticut Shotgun Manufacturing Co. in New Britain, Connecticut, makes a high-grade Fox shotgun. Next on the punch list is the LeFever. These were expensive even before they became collectible. The Daniel LeFever patented the first true hammerless shotgun in 1883. The L.C. Smith had the unique distinction of being the only American sidelock. Built from 1890–1945 the guns are sought after by collectors. Starting in 1945, when Marlin took over manufacturing, the Smith lost a bit of appeal. Winchester's Model 21 is legendary for its strong action and though it does not have the storied tradition of the Parkers, Foxes, and Smiths, shooters have loved them since 1931 through the end of production in 1960. Ruger's Gold Label was announced in 2002 with

Below: The DE grade A.H. Fox is currently manufactured by Connecticut Shotgun Manufacturing Co. It is known for its fine workmanship and excellent shooting qualities.

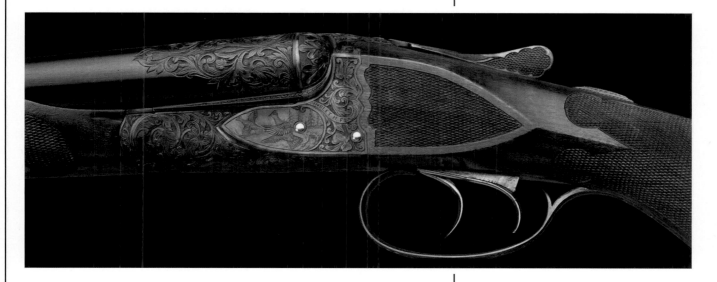

much fanfare that the American double was back. It was until Ruger figured it was too darn costly to build and nixed it from their catalog.

Colt Single Action Army

The Peacemaker
Produced: 1873–1941 (Gen 1), 1956–1974 (Gen 2), 1976–present (Gen 3)

The gunfight at the O.K. Corral never actually occurred at the Old Kindersley Corral in Tombstone, Arizona Territory. It really happened off Fremont Street in an alley adjacent to an open lot that abutted the rear of the corral. Hollywood and dime novels would have us believe there was a meeting at high noon; white hat heroes against black hat villains. The core of the gunfight was keeping the peace, and the "Peacemaker" was one of the common names used for the Colt Model P.

The fight was between two groups of men who detested each other. On one side were the outlaws and on the other the lawmen. As years passed facts surrounding the gunfight have taken on a subjective patina. The lawmen were of course the Earp brothers—Virgil, Wyatt, and Morgan—who made a living running saloons and gaming tables among other business endeavors. They were also lawmen in towns that sprung up in the west that are best described as in between the edge of civilization and pure wilderness. Doc Holliday was with the Earps that day, and Holliday was known more as a gambler than a dentist. The outlaws were cowboys who smuggled cattle and stole horses—rustlers by any other name. Their names were Billy Clanton and brothers Tom and Frank McLaury. Threats were made and there were pistol whippings the morning of the gunfight. The cowboys were carrying firearms, but a city ordinance prohibited possession of weapons in town. Virgil Earp, a Deputy US Marshal, decided to disarm the cowboys to keep the peace. When the two groups met at about 3:00 p.m. on Wednesday, October 26, 1881, two shots were fired. No one really knows who fired first. In thirty seconds it was over. Billy Clanton and the McLaury brothers were killed. Virgil and Morgan Earp were wounded. Pried from Billy's still warm dead hand was a Colt Single Action Army (SAA). Frank McLaury carried a similar Colt. A Colt SAA owned by Wyatt was auctioned in 2014 and fetched $225,000. It is not known if this Colt was used in the infamous gunfight. Today the gunfight is replayed every day; show times are held at noon, 2, and 3:30 p.m.

This legendary gunfight, like the Colt SAA, is part of the American fabric—as American as baseball, canned beer, pickup trucks, and apple pie. Deep down all Americans have a bit of cowboy or cowgirl in them. This is what makes this revolver so significant today though it was introduced in the late nineteenth century. When debuted it was innovative, and today it is a classic.

Samuel Colt was long in the cemetery when the 1873 first appeared. Colt, the man, had died in 1862. He had seen the tremendous success of his Walker revolver evolve into the success of 1852 Navy revolver and others. Colt was the consummate marketer and was quick to put a Colt revolver in the hands of people who held sway over the public's perception as well as government coffers; everyone from sultans to sheriffs received gifts of revolvers from Colt. It was a well-known brand and still ranks as one of the more recognizable brands in the world.

In the late 1800s the cutting edge high-tech weapon development was the metallic cartridge. Smith & Wesson held the rights to produce revolvers with a bored through cylinder which were capable of accepting metallic cartridges. The patent was in the name of Rollin White. Colt, the company, did not want to pay royalties to their competitor, so they modified old percussion revolver designs to accept metallic cartridges and called these conversion revolvers. While Colt waited for the patent to expire—the United States government actually denied Rollin an extension of his patent—their engineers who had created the conversion revolvers—William Mason and Charles Richards, worked on a totally new revolver design with the endgame being a United States government contract. The service revolver trials of 1872 held by the military showed the new Colt design a rugged and reliable revolver and the Single Action Army (SAA) was adopted by the United States government and put into service in 1873.

The Colt SAA purchased by the government featured a 7.5-inch barrel and was chambered in .45 Long Colt (LC) or .45 Colt, which was a new round to go with the new revolver. It was a very potent cartridge at the time and helped establish the .45 caliber as America's favorite pistol cartridge. The SAA, as its name states, is single-action. The hammer must be thumbed back and cocked to fire the revolver. The cylinder holds six rounds and is loaded via a loading gate on the right side of the pistol. The SAA was finished with a blued barrel, cylinder, and grip frame. The frame was case-hardened, which gave it a frothy mix of color. The Government model, also called the Cavalry model, had a smooth walnut grip. True Government models have the cartouche of government inspectors; the initials of David F. Clark, Orville Wood Ainsworth, or Henry Nettleton were stamped in the wood grip on the left side.

Collectors can instantly determine the generation of a Colt SAA. They may even hotly debate the actual number of Colt SAA generations, but it is generally agreed there are three. First Gen Colts were made from 1873–1941 and had a screw in the front of the frame to hold the cylinder or base pin in place. The screw could get lost and threads could loosen. Later generations used a spring-loaded base pin screw that is pressed to remove the base pin. A cylinder or base pin bushing eased operation with blackpowder loads. Original .45 LC cartridges were loaded with blackpowder, which leaves a residue that can quickly bind a cylinder and make the weapon unusable. The cylinder is beveled at the front to aid in holstering. Sights are fixed. The rear consists of a groove milled in the top of the frame and the front is a squared-off rounded blade. The rear sight is a V-shaped groove. Some inexpensive copies of Colt SAAs do not shoot to point of aim, thus requiring the front sight to be bent or filed down. Flat springs are used throughout the SAA. Bill Ruger in the 1950s reengineered the SAA using a cast frame and coil springs and called it the Blackhawk. Coil springs have a far longer, if not infinite, life compared with the flat springs.

The SAA is slow to load and unload, because as each cartridge is loaded into a chamber, the cylinder rotates and loading continues. To unload is just as tedious, as each empty cartridge case needs to be ejected separately. To load it the hammer is pulled back to half cock, which allows the operator to swing open the loading gate and rotate the cylinder. The SAA has an ejector rod attached to the right side of the barrel to help eject sticky cases especially after extended fire with blackpowder cartridges. The S&W Model 3 Schofield, a direct competitor to the SAA at the time, is a break-top revolver that quickly unloads empty cases in one step. It was also quicker to reload than the Colt, but in the end the Schofield fired a less powerful round and was more delicate than the SAA.

The Colt SAA was used during the American Indian Wars on both sides; Native Americans often picked up revolvers and other weapons from fallen soldiers. Colt's major competitor at the time was Smith & Wesson. The Government purchased some Schofields and used both weapons. The Colt was soon the preferred weapon over the S&W. The Colt SAA served well in battle but by 1893 the Colt SAA was replaced by a newer Colt, the .38-caliber Colt M1892 Double Action Army Revolver with swing-out cylinder and double-action and single-action trigger. It was very similar to modern day revolvers. On paper it was cutting edge weaponry at the time, but in use the power from the .38 LC cartridge was anemic. During the three-month-long Spanish–American War, Teddy Roosevelt personally requested that Colt SAAs be taken out of mothballs for his Rough Riders. Between 1895 and 1906 the United States government had Springfield Armory in Massachusetts and the Colt factory in Connecticut rework over 16,000 Colt SAA Cavalry revolvers. The letter from the US Ordnance Department stated:

> "It is intended to shorten the barrels of all the .45-caliber Colt's revolvers on hand to a length of 5.5 inches [Cavalry models had 7-1/2-inch barrels] as provided for the 250 revolvers which you have been directed to prepare and issue to the batteries of light artillery. This alteration for the new revolvers (caliber .45) on hand can, it is thought, be done at the Armory, whilst those requiring renovation may be altered at the least expense to the Government by the Colt's Arms Company at the same time with the work of renovation to be done under the contract of Aug. 20, 1895, with that company."

This is how the reworked SAAs became known as Artillery models as the refurbished guns were to be issued to artillery troops. Some of these old SAAs had seen about twenty years of hard service during the Indian Wars while others were in storage and had never been used. The US Ordnance Department specified that Colt rework the used guns, and the guns in storage would be reworked by Springfield Armory. Original Artillery models, specifically those reworked by Springfield Armory have mismatched serial numbers as Springfield disassembled the guns and grouped similar parts together. No effort was made to keep serial numbered parts together and the government saved on the cost because of this practice.

Later in 1899 during the Philippine–American War, the SAAs saw additional service. Troops needed firepower to deal with Moro tribesmen. The Moros proved to be vicious fighters wielding spears and bolo knives who worked themselves up to such fervor that troops found the stopping power of the .45 LC was the only solution in hand-to-hand combat. After this second war and the repeated experience of the shortcomings of .38 LC, the US government embarked on finding a new caliber. The 45 ACP and 1911 pistol were not too far in the near future. By 1902 the Colt SAA was finally retired, but that is not to say the Colt SAA has not seen other wars. General George S. Patton carried an engraved and ivory handle Colt SAA during World War II in the European Theater.

For the civilian market Colt offered the SAA in various barrel lengths: 4.75, 5.5, and 7.5 inches were most common. Shorter-barreled models were known as the Sheriff's Model, Storekeeper, or Banker's Special.

Perhaps the most famous and oddest variant of the Colt SAA is the Buntline, a standard SAA revolver with a 12-inch barrel (or longer). As the tale about who invented and who used the Buntline has grown grander and more embellished over the years, decades, and centuries, so, too, has the length of the revolver's barrel grown. Some Buntlines have barrels 16 or 18 inches in length. The Buntline is usually associated with Wyatt Earp due to a fictionalized biography of Earp written in 1931 by Stuart Lake and titled *Wyatt Earp: Frontier Marshal*. Lake describes Earp using a long-barreled Buntline, but there is no direct evidence to support that Earp ever used or even owned a Buntline revolver. What is known or alleged is that a late nineteenth century dime novelist with the pseudonym of Ned Buntline had the revolvers specifically made and presented to famous lawmen at the time, and Earp is alleged to have received one of these long-barreled revolvers. Ned Buntline was actually the pen name of Edward Zane Carroll Judson, who wrote four dime novels, all about the exploits of Buffalo Bill.

The Colt Flattop Target model featured an adjustable rear sight and an interchangeable front sight blade. The top strap of the frame was flat, hence the name Flattop. Another variant also used for target shooting was the Bisley, named after a famous target range in Bisley, England. The Bisley is unique in that it had a long, bent grip and different hammer and trigger, making it better suited for the target shooting style of the late nineteenth century. The Colt Frontier Six-Shooter model (the civilian variant of the Military SAA) was chambered in .44-40 WCF, the same caliber Winchester debuted in the Model 1873 lever-action rifle. The round proved so popular with shooters and hunters, Colt was forced to chamber their SAA in the round. Cowboys of the day liked the convenience of using the same cartridge in their rifle and revolver. Today they are all generically called SAAs.

Colt purists and collectors know which generation had a rounded or a squared trigger guard as well as the numerous other characteristics that separate different generations. During World War II Colt ceased production of the SAA to build other weapons ordered by the government, namely the Colt 1911 semiautomatic pistol. Production resumed in 1956 ushering in the Second Gen Colt SAAs. In the 1950s westerns were a TV show staple—*Have Gun – Will Travel*, *Gunsmoke*, *The Big Valley*, *Bonanza*, *Bret Maverick*, and a herd of others. It was a good opportunity to sell SAA revolvers, and companies like Great Western Arms Company, which produced the first SAA clones from 1954–1964, and Sturm, Ruger and Company, which began manufacturing SAAs in .22 rimfire in 1953. SAAs from Germany and Belgium were also produced, but like Great Western Arms, they all rode off into the sunset. Today Colt and Ruger in the United States and Uberti and Pietta in Italy still produce SAA revolvers. The Italians probably have produced more SAAs than Colt ever did. During Colt's Second Generation span the New Frontier was offered;—a SAA with a fully adjustable rear sight and ramp front sight. Ruger's Blackhawk had similar sights on their revolvers, and many shooters liked the adjustable sights. Colt's Third Gen began in 1976 and continues to this day. As

Above: Wyatt Earp later in life and well into the twentieth century still carried a Colt SAA.

Middle: Predecessors to the SAA were Colt conversion revolvers; this is a reproduction from Uberti of a Colt 1872 Army.

Below: Old print advertisement for the Colt Frontier Six-Shooter, retail price $34.00.

Retail Price: $34.00
Dealers Price: $27.20
  For the Following Cartridges
.32-20. (.32 Winchester.)
.38-40. (.38 Winchester.)
.38 Colt Special. (Using .38 Long Colt, .38 Short Colt, also .38 S. & W. Special, Full and Mid Range Loads.)
.44 Russian and .44 S. & W. Special.
.44-40. (.44 Winchester.) **.45 Colt.**

Colt Single Action Army Revolver

SIX SHOTS.
LENGTHS OF BARREL. 4¾, 5½ and 7½ inches.

FINISH. Case Hardened Frame; Blued Barrel and Straps, or Full Nickel Plated. Rubber Stocks.

WEIGHT. .45 Caliber. With 4¾-inch barrel, 37 ounces.
LENGTH OVER ALL. With 4¾-inch barrel, 10¼ inches.

Above: This Colt was factory-engraved by Cuno Helfricht and shipped to Albuquerque, NM, in 1893. Courtesy Hmaag.

the generations evolved Colt made slight modifications to the SAA design and in Third Gen guns changes—like a new cylinder bushing—were made to ease manufacturing and make it more cost effective. The cylinder bushing was subsequently changed back to the original style.

Left: The Bisley used the same style action as the SAA but featured a different grip angle.

The SAA is a natural pointer. The balance is near perfect. No wonder trick shooters, exhibitionists, and fast draw shooters like the late Bob Munden can make the SAA sing and spin around their trigger fingers. Even B-movie

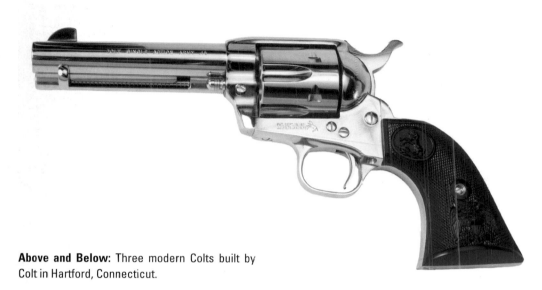

Above and Below: Three modern Colts built by Colt in Hartford, Connecticut.

Johnny Baker.

Above: Photographs of cowboys from the Old West proudly showing off their Colt hardware.

western extras make it look easy to use the SAA. Thumb back the hammer and the Colt SAA has four distinct clicks. Music to some ears.

The Colt SAA is one of the most recognizable revolvers in the world. On one end of the spectrum the SAA is a cowboy's tool. It is hard to find a pristine example of an early First Gen for the simple fact these revolvers were used day in and day out. On the other end of the spectrum, the SAA is a blank canvas for the engraver. Emigrants from Europe who worked in the Colt factory like Gustave Young, Louis Daniel Nimschke, Cuno Helfricht, and others created stunning and beautiful works of art out of the Colts. Cowboy Action Shooting in recent years has introduced the Colt SAA to many new shooters who dress up in period costume and plug away at steel and cardboard target desperadoes.

Leave an Empty Chamber

Since the SAA does not have a built-in safety, the hammer should always rest on an empty chamber. That way, if the revolver is accidentally dropped it will not discharge. To load a Colt SAA (and Italian knock-offs), load one cartridge, skip a chamber, and load the rest of the chambers. This best loading practice ensures the hammer rests on an empty chamber. It also means the six-shooter is really a five-shooter.

Left: Load one, skip one, then fill the remaining chambers. This allows a user to rest the hammer on an empty chamber for safety.

Specifications
CALIBER: .32-20 WCF, .38-40 WCF, .38 Short Colt, .38 Long Colt, .38 Colt Special, .38 S&W Special, .357 Magnum, .41 Long Colt, .44 Russian, .44 S&W Special, .44-40 WCF, .45 Long Colt (over 30 different calibers in total)
BARREL LENGTH: 4.75, 5.5, and 7.5 inches (most common)
OA LENGTH: 10.25 inches (4.75-inch barrel)
WEIGHT: 37 ounces (4.75-inch barrel)
STOCK: Smooth wood or checkered rubber
SIGHTS: Fixed, groove rear/blade front
ACTION: Single-action
FINISH: Case-hardened frame/blue barrel, grip, and cylinder or nickel
CAPACITY: 6

Spaghetti Colts

Spaghetti Westerns are Western movies like *The Good, The Bad, and The Ugly*, *A Fistful of Dollars*, and others. Italian director Sergio Leone directed American actors on a set in Spain. Italian firearms manufacturers like Uberti and Pietta filled the demand for revolvers like the Colt SAAs for decades by producing low cost, good-quality copies. These "Spaghetti Colts" look and feel very close to original Colts. *Non male* even if it does not have a rampant colt on the side nor is it roll marked Hartford, Connecticut.

Below: Great Western manufactured a reproduction of the Colt SAA in 1954; numerous examples were used in TV and films.

The Duke's Final Six-Shooter

In John Wayne's final movie, *The Shootist*, he used a pair of Great Western Arms Co. elaborately engraved SAAs with ivory grips. The Great Western was the first American-made SAA knock-off. When Ruger started to produce the Blackhawk SAA, they literally put Great Western out of business.

GREAT WESTERN SINGLE ACTIONS

LARGE CALIBER

COMPLETE

REVOLVERS

Choice of Barrel Length 4¾" 5½" 7½"

CHOICE OF 8 CALIBERS

.357 Magnum
.45 ACP Caliber
.44-40 Caliber
.44 Magnum
.22 Caliber
.38 Special
.44 Special
.45 Long Colt

ONE PRICE ONLY $84.95

Mfg. in U.S.A. All Steel Construction, Blue Finish, Stag Grips, 100% Guaranteed.

GREAT WESTERN GUN KITS

FINISH IT YOURSELF and SAVE $$$

Easy to assemble. All machine operations have been completed. Only assembly of small parts remains to be done. All calibers & barrel lengths shown above are available.

ONE LOW PRICE $69.95

DEALERS SEND FOR INFORMATION

GREAT WESTERN ARMS SALES CO., Dept. O, 12438 Ventura Blvd., No. Hollywood, Calif.

Winchester Model 1873

The Gun That Won the West
Produced: 1873–1919, 2013–Present (Winchester); 1991–Present (reproductions)

The story of the Winchester 1873 rifle really began in 1860 with the Henry, a rifle that provided extreme firepower at a time when single-shot muzzle-loading rifles were common. The Henry also utilized a new development in ammunition, the metallic cartridge case. Benjamin Tyler Henry designed the rifle bearing his name. It was a breechloading, repeating rifle that used a manually operated lever to chamber and eject .44 rimfire cartridges. Though other repeating rifles like the Spencer Repeater were in use, the Henry changed the way the American Civil War was fought. Most soldiers on either side carried smooth bore, muzzle-loading muskets that had an effective range of about 100 yards and were slow to reload. The lever-action Henry was accurate due to a rifled barrel, and it had fast follow-up shots due to the lever-action mechanism. The Henry was manufactured with a brass frame, although some were made from iron, and a 24-inch barrel. The Union Army purchased the brass-framed Henry rifles and issued them to cavalry troops making the troops a fast moving force with plenty of firepower. Confederate troops came to call the Henry "that damn Yankee rifle you load on Sunday and shoot all week." With a magazine capacity of 16 rounds it was a formidable piece of weaponry.

Oliver Winchester was a major investor in the New Haven Arms Company, where the Henry was built, and when the company came upon hard times, Winchester, the consummate businessman, snapped up the company and renamed it Winchester Repeating Arms. Winchester had on staff Nelson King, who designed a side-loading gate eliminating one of the Henry rifle's weak spots, the magazine tube and loading system. The Henry is loaded via a barrel sleeve. First a spring-loaded follower under the rifle is compressed toward the muzzle and the barrel sleeve is rotated open to expose the magazine tube where cartridges are dropped in base first. Spring tension pushes the rounds into the receiver. The system is awkward to load and delicate as the magazine tube and barrel sleeve could become dented and render the rifle useless. Oliver Winchester and Nelson King had other plans and that plan took the form of the first Winchester rifle—the Model 1866, the predecessor of the Winchester Model 1873. The Winchester Model 1866 was commonly referred to as a "Yellow Boy" as it used a brass frame similar to the Henry rifle. It also shared the same caliber, .44 rimfire. King added a forend on the new rifle and sealed off the magazine tube.

Firearm and ammunition development at the time in 1873 was going gangbusters. Colt had debuted the Single Action Army revolver in .45 Colt for military use in 1873. The Colt was a well-built, rugged revolver chambered in a new centerfire cartridge—.45 Long Colt—that at the time was proprietary to Colt. Winchester on the other hand debuted the Model 1873 rifle and a new cartridge: the .44-40 Winchester and American shooters were changed forever. The Model 1873 was a new lever-action design, much stronger—the receiver was manufactured from steel rather than brass—and it was chambered in a new caliber, too, the .44 WCF (Winchester Centerfire), more commonly known as the .44-40. The round used a .44 caliber bullet, the ".44" part of the cartridge name, and 40 grains of blackpowder, the "-40" designation in the name. If there ever was a legendary rifle the Winchester 1873 is that rifle. The popularity of the rifle and the caliber were unmatched by any other firearm maker at the time. In fact Colt was forced to chamber their SAA revolver in .44-40 due to the caliber's popularity. The civilian model of the SSA, called the Colt Frontier Six-Shooter, was offered in .44-40 because civilian customers demanded a revolver in a caliber that matched their Winchester 1873. Competing rifle manufacturers like Marlin and Whitney also chambered their rifles in the new cartridge.

Cowboys liked the convenience of having a rifle and revolver chambered in the same caliber since it meant having to buy only one type of ammunition. There was a dearth of convenience stores in the old west and one-room general stores—the department stores of the day—were few and far between. Thus having a rifle and pistol share the same ammo made sense. Outlaws, Native Americans, lawmen, hunters, and settlers all used the Model 1873 and the .44-40 cartridge as did the military. This is the rifle that coined the saying "The gun that won the west." The caliber/rifle combination offered good accuracy and power to kill game the size of whitetail deer and mule deer efficiently. Frank Barnes in *Cartridges of the World* surmises the .44-40 cartridge has killed more game—and people—than any other cartridge.

Specifications

CALIBER: .22 Rimfire, .32-20 WCF, .38-40 WCF, 44-40 WCF (originals); .38 Special/.357 Magnum, .45 Long Colt (modern reproductions)

BARREL LENGTH: 14, 15, 16, 20, 24, and 30 inches

OA LENGTH: 49.3 inches (30-inch barrel)

WEIGHT: 9.5 pounds (30-inch barrel)

STOCK: Smooth oil-finished wood (standard)

SIGHTS: Adj. notch rear/fixed post front

ACTION: Lever-action

FINISH: Case-hardened frame/blue barrel

CAPACITY: 9, 10, 13, or 15 (depending on barrel length and caliber)

The Winchester factory in New Haven, Connecticut, manufactured over 720,000 Model 1873 repeating rifles between 1873 and 1919. Originally it was chambered only in .44-40, then in .38-40 and .32-20 and .22 rimfire. Even though newer lever-action rifles were developed and sold (for example, the Model 1876, Model 1892, and Model 1894), the Model 1873 was extremely popular and produced well into the twentieth century. Modern replicas made in Italy of stronger steel allow the '73 to now be chambered in .38 Special/.357 Magnum and .45 Colt. Italian firearms manufacturers like Uberti have been manufacturing Model 1873 clones since the 1990s. Companies like Cimarron, EMF Company, Navy Arms, and Taylor's & Co. have been importing reproduction rifles to fill modern cowboy needs. These newer reproductions might not have "New Haven, Connecticut" roll marked on the barrel but they re-create the flavor of the bygone era. With crescent steel butt plates, blued or frothy case-hardened colors, modern 1873s are beautiful rifles—and life is too short to shoot an ugly rifle. Just like back in the day when Winchester was manufacturing rifles in New Haven, Connecticut, a multitude of custom options are available like checkered wood pistol grip stocks, and octagon or round barrels. Originals were built in three types: carbines, rifles, and muskets. Some of the deluxe models are highly valued by collectors.

With a lot of shooters channeling their inner cowboy the 1873 has seen resurgence, not that it ever faded away. Western movies and TV shows have fostered the cowboy in all of us with Cowboy Action Shooting taking it to a whole other level with guys and gals dressing the part of old west characters and competing in shooting competitions where reproduction Winchester rifles, among other types of reproductions, are used to shoot at cardboard and steel desperadoes.

Above: Since 2010, Winchester is again offering the Model 1873 in a variety of configurations like this short rifle with a 20-inch round barrel.

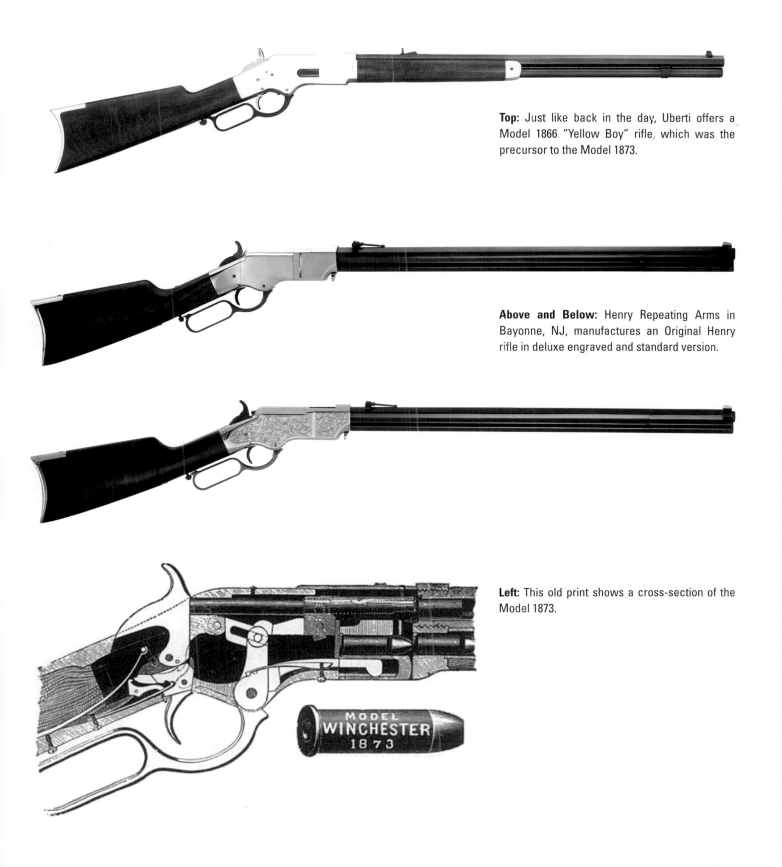

Top: Just like back in the day, Uberti offers a Model 1866 "Yellow Boy" rifle, which was the precursor to the Model 1873.

Above and Below: Henry Repeating Arms in Bayonne, NJ, manufactures an Original Henry rifle in deluxe engraved and standard version.

Left: This old print shows a cross-section of the Model 1873.

MODEL
WINCHESTER
1873

Right: These Texas Rangers show off their Winchester Model 1873 rifles circa mid-1880s.

Below: A cowboy action shooting competitor puts a Model 1873 through its paces; note the empty cases in the air. Courtesy SASS.

"One of One Thousand"

In 1875 Winchester offered a special run of rifles called Model 1873 "One of One Thousand." These rifles were finely crafted with deluxe walnut stocks, bluing, and case-hardening. At the time the rifle cost about $100. Today an original "One of One Thousand" depending on the condition will fetch anywhere from $75,000 to $500,000. Only 136 were manufactured.

Hollywood Glitz, Winchester Sizzle

The 1950 black and white movie *Winchester '73* starred Jimmy Stewart in the lead role with Shelly Winters, Dan Duryea, and Stephen McNally supporting. The story is about a prized Winchester Model 1873 rifle that passes through the hands of various owners. The Writers Guild of America nominated the film for Best Written American Western.

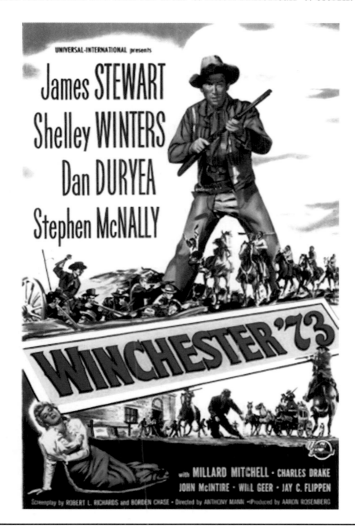

Left: In 1950 Universal Studios released *Winchester '73* starring Jimmy Stewart and a prized Winchester Model 1873.

Super-Sized Model 1873

In 1876 Winchester debuted the Model 1876, also known as the Centennial Model, since it came out during our country's Centennial celebration. Chambered in what was then a high power rifle cartridge, the .45-75 Winchester, the cartridge had similar ballistics as the .45-70 Government cartridge. The Model 1876 used a longer and heavier frame than the Model 1873 and was popular with hunters, including Teddy Roosevelt, who hunted with a custom Model 1876 that was elaborately engraved. Other big-bore calibers the Winchester was chambered in included the .40-60 Winchester, .45-65 Winchester, and .50-95 Express.

Above: Uberti makes a reproduction of the Model 1876 with a 28-inch barrel that weighs 10 pounds.

Right: When Teddy Roosevelt played cowboy he used a custom Model 1876; that knife tucked in his belt was from Tiffany & Co.

Westley Richards & Co. Boxlock

Boxlock from Birmingham
Produced: 1875–Present

Westley Richards & Co. has been making unique and especially good shotguns and rifles for over two hundred years, but in 1875 two of their gunsmiths, Anson and Deeley, created a simple yet elegant lock mechanism for a hammerless action. The hammers are actually concealed inside the action making the double shotgun or rifle streamlined. At the time of its creation, external hammer guns were all the rage and this new type of action shook the old school gunmakers of England.

The new action used the top lever to open the action, and that in turn allowed the barrels of the gun to pivot down thus cocking the shotgun. No need to thumb back the external hammers, which was the common mechanism at the time.

Above: Current manufacture of a Westley Richards double rifle using a boxlock action. Courtesy Westley Richards & Co.

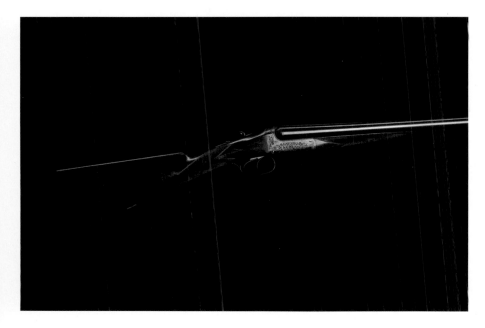

Left: Westley Richards Heronshaw 12-gauge boxlock made around 1938. Courtesy Westley Richards & Co.

This new action required fewer parts, was simpler to manufacture, and was the moment the double-barrel shotgun transitioned into a modern gun.

As a custom gunmaker, Westley Richards & Co.'s list of custom options is extensive. Therefore, I have not provided an extensive specifications section for this particular firearm.

Right: Cross-section drawing of the boxlock action.

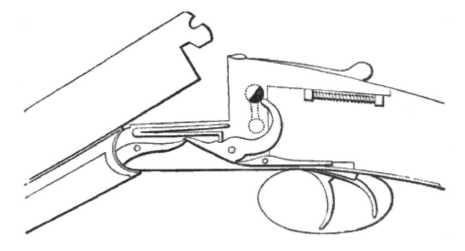

Right: Classic Anson and Deeley boxlock in a Westley Richards & Co. manufactured gun.

Purdey Self-Opener

Best for a Reason
Produced: 1879–Present

The epitome of British side-by-side shotguns is perhaps best represented by James Purdey & Sons of London. All guns are custom-made and cost a king's ransom, but the marriage of wood and steel is truly magnificent and results in a work of functioning art. The term "Best Gun" is used to describe a Purdey double-barrel shotgun of the finest quality. A Purdey will fit its owner like a finely tailored suit. The momentous breakthrough at Purdey came when one of their employees, Frederick Beesley, invented the self-opening action system. The self-opener uses the residual energy of the mainspring to open the gun and eject the spent shell. Purdey shotguns and double rifles have been built on this action ever since.

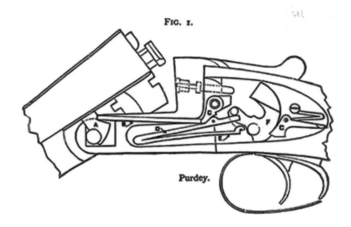

Above: A drawing of the Beesley action shows the inventive way the springs open the action.

Above: Sideplates from a recently manufactured double rifle show elaborate engraving and the finest workmanship.

Marlin Golden Model 39A

Oldest and Longest Continuously Produced Rimfire Rifle Produced: 1891–Present

Built from forged steel and sculpted from American ground black walnut, the Marlin Golden Model 39A is the latest variation of one of the oldest and continuously produced rimfire rifles in United States history. This rifle is renowned for its excellent lever action and accuracy. Many a small game hunter and backyard plinker have used the Marlin 39A. In fact many times these rifles exchange hands in families with each successive generation. The 39A is a perfect example of a full size rimfire rifle. Many new shooters cut their teeth on a 39A shooting at tin cans. It is considered one of the finest examples of a lever-action .22 rimfire rifle and has been popular since introduction and a best-selling rifle for Marlin.

The Model 39A started life in 1891 as the Model 1891. This was the first lever-action rifle chambered for .22 LR. Later generations of the Model 1891, such as the Model 1892 and Model 1897 (a takedown version), led to the Model 39 that came out in 1921 and the Model 39-A in 1937. Minor engineering and manufacturing tweaks differentiate the models over the years, and the Model 39A originally debuted as the Golden Mountie Model 39A in 1954 and featured a gold-plated trigger. In the 1950s the biggest change was Micro-Groove rifling, Marlin's proprietary rifling. By 1983 a cross-bolt safety was added, and ever since the 39A has been virtually unchanged.

The 39A uses the Marlin characteristic side-ejection flat-top receiver. This receiver style allows the easy mounting of an optic. The lever-action is fed via a tubular magazine. An inner tube is rotated and pulled from the magazine tube enough to allow cartridges to be inserted into the loading port. Like most lever-actions the 39A has an exposed hammer that allows a user to manually cock the hammer to fire the rifle. Current models have a rebounding hammer, which means after the hammer strikes the firing pin it automatically rebounds to a position off the firing pin. This feature ensures that the rifle will not accidentally fire if dropped on the hammer. The 39A is also designed as a takedown rifle.

Below: The current Model 39A is a swift pointing rifle with the heft of a center-fire rifle and with tack-driving accuracy.

Loosen the takedown screw located on the right side of the receiver and the stock and lever mechanism separate from the receiver and barrel. This makes cleaning the 39A easier.

Every shooter should have some trigger time with a Marlin Model 39A. You will not be disappointed.

Little Sure Shot

Annie Oakley was an amazing exhibition shooter and a shooting super star who appeared in Buffalo Bill's Wild West shows. Lakota tribal chief Sitting Bull, who was also a member of the Buffalo Bill's show for a time, gave Oakley the nickname *Wantanya Cicilia,* which translated means "Little Sure Shot." One of her most famous shooting feats was performed on March 10, 1893, when she used a Marlin Model 1891 loaded with .22 Short ammunition to shoot one jagged hole into the center of an ace of hearts playing card off-hand, from a distance of 12 yards. Oakley fired the 25 shots in just 27 seconds. Oakley was as popular as any pop singer in modern times and an advocate for female rights and felt it was important for women to learn how to shoot firearms.

Specifications
CALIBER: .22 Short, Long, Long Rifle
BARREL LENGTH: 24 inches
OA LENGTH: 40 inches
WEIGHT: 6.5 pounds
STOCK: Checkered American Black Walnut (current production)
SIGHTS: Adjustable semi-buckhorn rear/ramp with brass bead front
ACTION: Lever-action
FINISH: Blued
CAPACITY: 26 (.22 Short), 21 (.22 Long), 19 (.22 Long Rifle)

Left: Annie Oakley was a trick shooter in Buffalo Bill's Wild West Show, and at times she used a Marlin 1891 to ply her shooting prowess.

Right: An old advertisement from Marlin touted the advantages of Micro-Groove rifling over traditional rifling.

Micro-Groove Rifling

In 1953 Marlin started to use proprietary Micro-Groove rifling in their .22 rimfire rifles. Unlike traditional cut rifling, Micro-Groove rifling has sixteen shallow grooves for less bullet distortion and a better gas seal.

Winchester Model 94

"The" Deer Rifle
Produced: 1894–2006, 2010–Present

When our grandfathers hunted deer, a deer rifle usually meant a .30-30 and often more specifically a Model 94. Winchester Model 94s were a common sight in the racks at deer camps. The best way to describe Model 94s is as pre-64 and post-64 model types. A design change took place in 1964 to make the Model 94 less expensive to manufacture. Some stampings replaced milled forgings, rolled pins replaced solid pins—Winchester purists cringed at the changes. With over five million Model 94s produced, the 94 was a very popular rifle. But purists will be purists. In 2006 the red brick Winchester building in New Haven, Connecticut, locked its doors for good. The Model 94 went dormant, but in 2010 Winchester began producing Model 94s again; the first was a gussied-up engraved model. I do miss "Made in New Haven, Connecticut" roll stamped on the barrel, but I'll settle for "Made in Japan" on the current Winchester Model 94 rifles. The new Winchester Model 94 is same as it ever was—sort of.

The lever-action mechanism of the Model 94 is complex compared to the Marlin 336. But the Model 94 is thinner, lighter, and a naturally fast on-target rifle. From its debut until about 1982 the Model 94 ejected empties upward making mounting a scope difficult. Either the scope was mounted to the left side of the receiver or forward of the receiver like on a scout rifle. In 1982 angle-eject was an option Winchester touted; empties were now flung to the right allowing hunter to mount a scope directly on top of the receiver. As the rifle broke in, the loop lever would sag but continue to operate smoothly. Lever guns are a lot like dungarees from thirty years ago. Both are stiff until broken in. A tubular magazine with right side loading gate held six rounds of 30-30 ammo on a 20-inch barrel variant In 1992 a cross bolt safety was added to the design to block the hammer. This of course made the rifle safer to use but also mucked up the looks of this classic.

The lever and lever mechanism in the twenty-first century model is closer to original models. Edges of the lever are

Below: This 1956 ad played on the western appeal of the Model 94.

Specifications

CALIBER: .25-35 Winchester, .30-30 Winchester (initial caliber), 7-30 Waters, .307 Winchester, .32-40 Winchester, .32 Winchester, .357 Magnum, .375 Winchester, .38-55 Winchester, .44 Magnum

BARREL LENGTH: 16, 20 (most common), 26 inches

OA LENGTH: 37.8 inches

WEIGHT: 6.8 pounds (20-inch barrel)

STOCK: Smooth walnut (most common)

SIGHTS: Adjustable semi-buckhorn rear/hooded bead ramp front

ACTION: Lever-action, exposed hammer

FINISH: Blued

CAPACITY: 6-round tubular magazine (20-inch barrel)

radiused and the lever loop is more oval, less bent, and kidney-shaped, and the underside of the bolt is more like originals. Round locking bolt trunnions and the underside of the bolt are more like originals, so articulating the lever of the new rifles is slick and smooth. The hammer on new rifles is also rebounding. No half-cock notch like pre-64s. A brand new feature on the newer variants is an articulated cartridge stop that helps avoid misfeeds or doubling cartridges. Some 94s had a way of chewing up the tip of softnose bullets. A buckhorn rear sight adjusts for elevation via a ladder and is drift adjustable for windage; it partners with a genuine Marble Arms front sight with a brass bead. Unlike many pre- and post-64s, there is no hood for the front sight. That's just as well since hoods had a habit of getting lost the first time they filled with snow or debris and caused a hunter to miss their buck. With an overall length of

Right: "Most popular game getter" is how the 94 is described in this 1956 ad.

38 inches and a weight of 6-3/4 pounds the Model 94 handles like models of yore. It is quick to the shoulder, maneuverable, and the action is smooth and easy to operate.

Top and Middle: Both the newer Short Rifle (top) and Carbine—yes, there is a difference—feature a round 20-inch barrel.

Above: Looking old school, the current Sporter model has a 26-inch barrel and checkered stock.

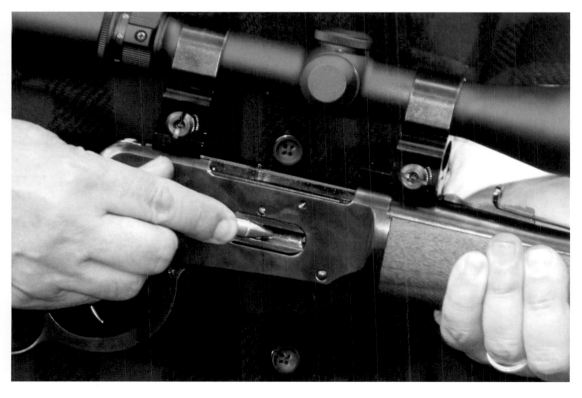

Left: The Model 94, combined with newer .30-30 ammo choices like this Hornady Flex-Tip ammo, is good to go for the next one hundred years.

First To Go Smokeless: .30 WCF

Back in 1895, the Model 94 lever-action rifle was built to use the new .30 WCF cartridge, or as it is better known, the .30–30—*treinta-treinta* south of the Rio Grande, "thurty-thurty" north of the Rio Grande. It was the first cartridge in the United States to use smokeless powder. The .30 WCF debuted with a 160-grain softpoint bullet and 30 grains of smokeless powder stoked to a muzzle velocity of 1,970 fps. It is a rimmed cartridge, which means there is a flange around the base of the cartridge that is used for two purposes: one is to head space the cartridge in the chamber, and the second is to extract the cartridge. The .30–30 nomenclature was the old way of describing rounds. The first number indicates the cartridge's caliber; the second indicates the grains of blackpowder. Even though the .30–30 used smokeless powder, the name stuck. For 116 years the .30–30 has been the yardstick by which all other deer cartridges are measured. It offers light recoil and is quite capable of killing whitetail deer and black bear–sized game out to two hundred yards. It would not be a first choice for elk, but tons of elk meat and antlers have been collected with the .30–30.

Below: Traditional rounds like the Winchester and Remington softpoints (left) are time-tested, while the Hornady and Federal cartridges give the .30-30 a high-tech boost.

Winchester Model 1897

Trench Sweeper, Duck Reaper
Produced: 1897–1957 (Winchester), 2006–Present (reproductions)

The reliability and ease of use, if not the ominous sound of a pump shotgun cycling, took a major step forward with the Winchester Model 1897 pump-action shotgun. From soldiers and law enforcement to hunters and competitive shooters the '97 ushered in the widespread use of pump-action shotguns during an era when blackpowder shells and shotguns were rapidly being replaced with smokeless shells and newer and stronger shotguns. At the turn of the twentieth century most shotguns were side-by-sides offering a fast two shots. Repeating shotguns like Winchester's Model 1888 lever-action provided more shell capacity and a faster operating mechanism, but it was the pump-action shotgun that became king of fast shooting, fast follow-up shots, and high shell capacity. To this day, pump-action shotguns are still in widespread use by countless police departments, hunters, competitive shooters, and home defenders. The Model 1897, though a bit clunky by today's pump-shotgun standard helped companies like Stevens, Remington, Mossberg, and others refine the design to its maximum potential.

The Winchester Model 1897 was the first pump-action shotgun designed for the then new smokeless powder shells. But it wasn't Winchester's first pump-action shotgun. John Browning had designed the Model 1893 pump-action shotgun, which was introduced in the same year. The 1893 and 1897 are very similar in appearance and operation; the Model 1893 used blackpowder shells. The Model 1893 was later reengineered to use smokeless shells, which are more powerful and create more chamber pressure. In essence the Model 1897 was a reworked Model 1893.

The Winchester 1897 pump- or slide-action shotgun features a tubular magazine directly under the barrel. The action is cycled by the user pumping or sliding the forend rearward, which ejects a fired shell and cocks the weapon. The forward movement of the forend chambers the round and locks the bolt into battery making the shotgun ready to fire. If the trigger is pressed while the forearm is pumped, the gun will fire. This is called a slam fire and allows the Model 97 to be rapid fired. The '97 has an exposed hammer so

Specifications
GAUGE: 12, 16 (2-3/4-inch shells)
BARREL LENGTH: 20 (riot), 22 (trench), 26–30 inches (commercial variants)
OA LENGTH: 39.2 inches (20-inch barrel)
WEIGHT: 8 pounds (20-inch barrel)
STOCK: Smooth wood/grooved forend (standard)
SIGHTS: Bead front
ACTION: Pump-action/exposed hammer
FINISH: Blued
CAPACITY: 5-round tube magazine

the operator can thumb back the hammer on a loaded chamber and shoot the weapon. Available in numerous barrel lengths, shooters had a choice of either 12- or 16-gauge and either a solid frame or takedown. Over one million of these shotguns were manufactured.

During World War I a trench version of the Model '97 was manufactured with a heat shield over the barrel and bayonet lug. It was used to clean out the trenches of enemy soldiers and was nicknamed the "trench sweeper." The weapon was so effective in the close hand-to-hand combat in the trenches that the Germans complained the weapon was too brutal for combat and did not follow the rules of war at that time. Needless to say the Model 1897 continued to serve in both world wars and was still in use during the Vietnam War.

Back home these shotguns were born to hunt. Market hunters used the Model 1897 to its full effect and wreaked havoc with game populations until market hunting was outlawed. For the typical hunter, however, the Model '97 was used on everything from duck, pheasant, and geese to grouse, quail,

Below: Here a cowboy action shooter exercises a Model 1897 on steel outlaws. Courtesy SASS.

and deer. The versatility of the shotgun cannot be underestimated; it can be loaded with shot or slugs depending on the game hunted. Law enforcement also found the '97 useful; a riot variant with a 20-inch barrel was used to keep the peace. Trapshooters—John Browning was a trapshooting enthusiast but used the Model 1893—found the Model 1987 in trap variants effective on the trap ranges.

Today many of these old '97s have been repurposed with their barrels cut down to compete in cowboy action shooting. I call that a great retirement for these old shotguns. Compared to modern pump-action shotguns the Model '97 is a complicated mechanism. Chinese-manufactured clones of Model '97 have been imported into United States specifically to meet the demand from cowboy action shooters though these shotguns lack the aura as well as the finish of the originals.

Above: This is a reproduction of the famed Model 1897; Cimarron, Taylor's & Co., EMF, and others import these clones.

Transition to Smokeless Powder

John Browning was not the first to develop the pump-action shotgun, but it could be argued that he designed a better pump-action, and Winchester began building them starting with the Model 1893. The Model 1893 used a blackpowder 12-gauge shell and was offered to the public just prior to the widespread change over to smokeless 12-gauge shells. Winchester thought it best to tweak the Model 1893 and so the Model 1897 was launched with John Browning's modifications. The concern Winchester had with the Model 1893 was a hunter or clay target shooter might accidentally load a smokeless shell in the Model 1893 gun. Though the shell lengths of the 12 gauge blackpowder load and smokeless load are different—the smokeless load is longer—there was the possibility of a smokeless round being fired in the Model 1893 and potentially destroying the shotgun and in turn harming or killing the user. When the 1897 debuted Winchester offered Model 1893 owners the chance to swap the older '93 model with the newer '97 model for no charge. Lesser liability for Winchester and a good deal for Model 1893 owners.

Thumb-Buster

You might have an old relative or neighbor or old-timer who might refer to the '97 as a thumb-buster and for good reason. When the action is cycled rearward the bolt protrudes from the receiver to cock the hammer and if your grip is too high on the stock your thumb will get bruised. Modern pump guns have a hammerless design where the hammer and bolt are actually inside the receiver away from unsuspecting thumbs.

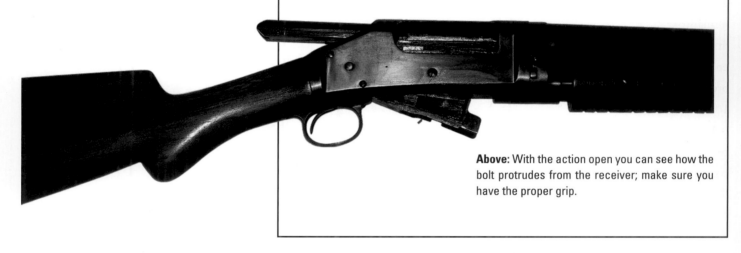

Above: With the action open you can see how the bolt protrudes from the receiver; make sure you have the proper grip.

Smith & Wesson Model 10

The Perfect 10
Produced: 1899–Present

The revolver has lost stature in this generation of polymer-framed semiautomatic pistols. The six-shot, double-action revolver, especially the Smith & Wesson Model 10, is unassuming because we take it for granted, enamored as we are with the latest and greatest technology. The Model 10 has proven itself a safe, powerful, and reliable handgun since 1899. The Model 10 is one of those weapons about which operators don't think twice. If it is loaded and the trigger is pulled, it will fire. The Model 10 is completely reliable; that's why it's the most popular centerfire revolver ever made. Some six million units have been built, some used by cops from coast to coast, by the Allied forces during World War II, and by those who demand a quality weapon to protect house and home.

In 1899 S&W released the Smith & Wesson .38 Hand Ejector Model of 1899. The revolver was introduced on a new medium-sized frame S&W named the K-frame. Previously S&W only manufactured large N-frame revolvers. This DA/SA revolver was a marvel of technology at a time when single-action revolvers were still popular. The Model of 1899 allowed the operator to pull the trigger to fire the revolver a quick six times or cock back the hammer to fire. It has near perfect balance in hand making it a natural pointer. The sights were fixed and rugged and most importantly shot to point of aim. And the revolver was a handy size—not too small or too large. The US Navy and Army ordered thousands. In 1902 S&W updated the design and renamed it the .38 Military & Police. In 1905 a hammer block was incorporated into the mechanism to avoid discharging a cartridge if the revolver was accidentally dropped.

The Victory Model was a parkerized Model 10 outfitted for war. During World War II Victory Models chambered in .38 Special with either a 4- or 5-inch barrel were used by the Allies. It was the standard issue for aircrews for the US Navy and Marines. Some models lasted in service into the 1990s. The use of the Model 10 was so widespread among police departments it has been said that 80 percent of departments were armed with Model 10 revolvers.

Revolvers were available in a slew of barrel lengths—2 to 6 inches—and came with either a round or square butt. The Model 10 was also chambered in a new cartridge at the time, the .38 Special. The US Military wanted a more powerful round than the .38 Long Colt, so S&W met the challenge and introduced the round in 1898. The round is one of the most popular revolver cartridges of all times known for its accuracy and manageable recoil. Over the years the power and velocity of the round has been increased and +P loads were developed in 1972.

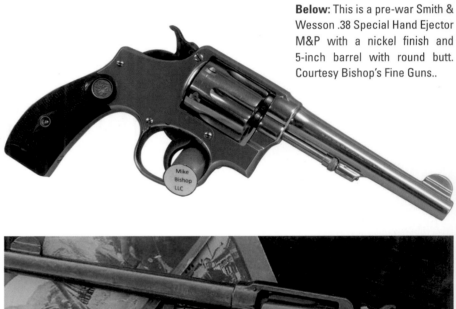

Below: This is a pre-war Smith & Wesson .38 Special Hand Ejector M&P with a nickel finish and 5-inch barrel with round butt. Courtesy Bishop's Fine Guns..

Above: The sights on the Model 10 are simple yet rugged.

Right: The Smith & Wesson .38 Hand Ejector Model of 1899 was the forerunner of the Model 10; this variant has a 6-inch barrel. Note the lack of an under lug, which was added to later models.

Specifications

CALIBER: .38 Long Colt, .38/200, .38 Special (most common)

BARREL LENGTH: 2, 2.5, 3, 4 (most common), 5, and 6 inches

OA LENGTH: 8.8 inches (4-inch barrel)

WEIGHT: 34 ounces (4-inch barrel)

STOCK: Checkered wood or textured rubber

SIGHTS: Fixed groove rear/blade front

ACTION: Single-action/double-action

FINISH: Blue (most common), nickel, or stainless

CAPACITY: 6

Top: This is an example of a Smith & Wesson .38 M&P model of 1905, the 4th change Target model with a 6-in. barrel and square butt. Courtesy of Bishops Fine Guns.

Middle: The Model 64 is a stainless steel version of the Model 10. Courtesy Smith & Wesson.

Bottom: Retro is cool and S&W offers the Model 10 through its Classic series of guns; this model has a round butt.

The FBI Load

In 1972 when .38 Special +P ammo was developed the FBI was looking for an effective .38 Special round. The FBI chose to load a 158-grain unjacketed, semi-wadcutter hollow-point soft lead bullet. The round was designed to rapidly expand in a soft target when fired from a 2- or 4-inch barreled revolver.

Top: The FBI Load uses an unjacketed, semi-wadcutter hollow-point bullet made of soft lead; this is a cross section of the bullet.

Bottom: Winchester Super X ammo is loaded to FBI specs with a muzzle velocity of 890 fps and 278 ft-lbs of muzzle energy.

Savage Model 99

The Savage Code: Bolt-Action Accuracy in a Lever-Action
Produced: 1899–1998

When I was young and uneducated in the ways of deer camp there was a rifle in the rack that had a lever but no hammer. The ability to silently cock back a hammer on a deer rifle was an art I was still perfecting, but this rifle made the task moot. When I was allowed to shoulder the rifle, I found the lever worked with a slickness nothing like a Marlin or Winchester or Stevens. The owner held out his hand, and in his palm were pointed bullets. Those can't work in a tubular magazine. But the rifle had no tubular magazine; it had a built-in box magazine. The rifle was a Savage Model 99, and at that moment it completely changed my notion of a lever-action rifle. This was back in the late 1970s, Savage had been changing the general hunting public's notion of what a lever-action rifle was since 1895.

In 1895 Arthur W. Savage introduced a hammerless lever-action rifle named the Model 1895. It was nothing like any lever-action rifle seen before. The Model 1895 was sleek and streamlined with no protruding hammer. It was called hammerless, but the hammer actually was housed inside the receiver. There was a cocking indicator, a small pin that protruded from the receiver that could be seen or felt, telling the user that the rifle was cocked. There was no tubular magazine as there was with all the previous lever-actions from Winchester, Marlin, and others. The Model 1895 used a five-shot rotary magazine which was designed with a spring-loaded, grooved spool that held each cartridge. The spool also held a counter so the user could easily see how many rounds were left in the magazine.

But the Model 1895's revelation was its spritzer-style bullets. Lever-actions were required to use flat- or round-nose bullets due to the tubular magazine. With the bullets loaded in line from bullet tip to primer in a lever-action, spitzer or pointed bullets were not used due to the possibility of the pointed bullet of one cartridge impacting the primer of the bullet in front of it and causing an accidental discharge. Spitzer bullets meant the rifle was more accurate and more powerful than its contemporaries. Savage actually claimed bolt-action accuracy in their lever-action rifles. Design changes to the Model 1895 led to the Model 1899 in 1899. By 1920 the rifle was simply called the Model 99.

Specifications

CALIBER: .22 Hi Power, .250 Savage, .22-250 Remington, .243 Winchester, .303 Savage, .30-40 Krag, .300 Savage, .30-30 Winchester, .308 Winchester, .32 Winchester Special, .358 Winchester, 7mm-08 Remington, .284 Winchester, .38-55 Winchester

BARREL LENGTH: 20, 22, 24, 26, and 28 inches

WEIGHT: 6.75 to 8.25 pounds (depending on barrel length/caliber)

STOCK: Wood/straight or pistol grip

SIGHTS: Adjustable semi-buckhorn rear/bead ramp front

ACTION: Lever-action/hammerless

FINISH: Blued

CAPACITY: 5-round rotary internal magazine/detachable magazine (later models)

Top: In 1965 Savage was touting the convenience of the debatable magazine in the Model 99.

Right: This old advertisement claimed "More power, speed, control" and that was not just marketing fluff; the Model 99 performed.

The rifle became a favorite with hunters across the country. As optics became more popular the Savage Model 99 was well-suited for their use, since it used a side eject action and the top of the receiver could be drilled and tapped to mount a scope. Many hunters installed an aperture or peep rear sight, making it a fast-to-aim rifle with an equally fast follow-up shot. The trigger was also better than other lever-action rifles at the time. Accuracy was excellent. In the 1960s a detachable magazine replaced the rotary magazine in an effort to help reduce manufacturing costs. The rotary magazine 99s are more desirable to collectors, but most deer or black bear hunters would take either model.

Speed Kills: .250-3000 Savage

The .250–3000 Savage, also called the .250 Savage, was the first commercially loaded American cartridge to break the 3000 fps speed barrier. Charles Newton, a firearms enthusiast, designed the cartridge to work in the Savage Model 99 rifle in 1915. An 87-grain spitzer bullet was used to achieve the speed, which completely amazed shooters at the time. The round was accurate, had a flat trajectory and was used to hunt everything from varmints to deer.

Left: Not many ammunition manufacturers still load the .250 Savage; these are some older 100-grain Silvertips from Winchester. Courtesy Dan Pazsint, Gunbroker.com Dealer Kingofcoins.

Medicine Gun: Winchester Model 1895

The Model 1895 completely changed the way Winchester thought about lever-action rifles. Featuring a fixed box magazine instead of a tubular magazine, the Model 1895 allowed Winchester to chamber the rifle in more powerful calibers that utilized spitzer bullets. The Winchester Model 1895 was used by several militaries including those of Russia and the United States. On safari in East Africa in 1909, Theodore Roosevelt used a Winchester Model 1895 chambered in the powerful .405 Winchester cartridge to hunt lion. Roosevelt called the rifle caliber combination his "medicine gun" for lions.

Above: The Model 1895 was Winchester's effort to create a lever-action compatible with spitzer or pointed bullets.

EARLY TWENTIETH CENTURY

Luger P08

First 9mm Pistol
Produced: 1900–1942; 1970s–1994 (post-war reproductions)

The Luger P08 is one of the most iconic and unique pistols ever manufactured. It features a toggle mechanism that was invented by Hugo Borchardt, who used the mechanism in the C-93 pistol in 1893. George Luger, a designer at Ludwig Lowe small arms factory in Berlin, Germany, radically redesigned the Borchardt toggle system and patented a new pistol design in 1898. The pistol is commonly called the Luger and holds the distinction as being one of the first successful military sidearms as well as being the first pistol chambered in 9mm. To this day the 9mm cartridge is the most popular handgun cartridge in use by most militaries, law enforcement agencies, and civilians around the world.

Some semiautomatic pistols of this era utilized an internal box magazine housed forward of the trigger guard, like the Mauser C96 and the Bergman-Bayard Model 1903. The John Browning–designed FN Browning M1900 and the Luger used a magazine housed in the grip of the pistol, which is how most modern handguns evolved. In operation the toggle and barrel assembly move rearward after a round is fired; the barrel is stopped by the frame, but the toggle continues and the knee joint of the toggle bends to extract the case and then moves forward to push a fresh round from the magazine into the chamber. In hand the comfortable grip angle of the Luger makes the pistol a natural pointer, easy for the operator to aim and get on target fast. The Luger is reliable when using high velocity cartridges that produce enough recoil to operate the mechanism.

The Luger was originally chambered in .30 Luger (7.62x21mm) and produced by Deutsche Waffen-und Munitionsfabriken (DWM) starting in 1900. At this time revolvers were the only type of handgun. Semiautomatic pistols at this time were radically new and most were awkward and complex. The Swiss Military was the first to adopt the pistol in 1900. The Germany Navy liked the

Specifications

CALIBER: 7.65x21mm Parabellum (.30 Luger), 9x19mm Parabellum (9mm)

BARREL LENGTH: 3.75–7.87 inches (4-in. most common)

OA LENGTH: 8.75 inches (4-inch barrel)

WEIGHT: 30.72 ounces (4-inch barrel)

GRIP: Checkered wood, plastic (war production)

SIGHTS: Fixed, notch rear/blade front

ACTION: Semiautomatic, short recoil-operated, toggle-locked

FINISH: Blued frame/barrel, straw controls

CAPACITY: 8-round magazine

Luger pistol but wanted a pistol with a more powerful round. Luger redesigned the .30 Luger cartridge in 1902 by resizing the bottleneck cartridge case to hold a larger bullet and creating the 9x19mm or 9mm Luger/Parabellum round. In 1904 the Imperial Germany Navy adopted the Luger chambered in 9mm with a 5.9-inch barrel and a two-position rear sight. The German Army was also keen on the new pistol and in 1908 accepted the Luger as the *Pistole 08* or P08. The P08 with a 3.9-inch barrel is perhaps the most common variant of the Luger. It served with the German Army during World War I and World War II. Shortly after the German adoption, other countries like Holland, Brazil, Bulgaria, Portugal, Russia, and others began using it. The US Army even considered the Luger, but adopted the M1911 instead. The P08 was manufactured by DWM (*Deutsche Waffen-und Munitionsfabriken*) and also by Erfurt, Mauser, Simon & Co., Krieghoff, and others. In 1994 a stainless steel variant bearing the Stoeger name was manufactured in Texas. Other firearm designs have copied the Luger grip angle, such as the Ruger Mark I (United States), Glisenti Model 1910 (Italy), Lahti Husqvarna Model 40 (Sweden), Lahti L-35 (Finland), and Nambu Type 14 (Japan) to name a few.

Like most semiautomatics of the time, the Luger required careful hand-fitting of parts; thus, manufacturing was expensive and time consuming. Nonetheless, Lugers are highly prized by collectors, with some variations considered more rare and coveted.

Opposite Page: Civilians were quick to adopt the new semiautomatic Luger, like this lawman in the late nineteenth century.

Right: The P08 was the first pistol to be chambered in 9mm, which is the most widely used and popular caliber in use today.

Right: The Luger was as popular with civilian shooters as it was with military and police.

Bottom Left: Lugers are coveted by collectors; this specimen costs some $5,000.00. Courtesy of Mitchell's Mausers.

Bottom Right: The rear back strap on some Luger models, like this one, allowed an operator to attach a shoulder stock.

Top: The Luger's contemporary was the Mauser C96, which had an internal box magazine loaded via a stripper clip, shown here with a wood shoulder stock that doubled as a holster. Courtesy M62.

Above Left: Some Texas Rangers in 1907 were fast to adopt the new Luger. Here Captain John H. Rogers holds a Luger. That's famous lawman Frank Hamer in the black hat holding a Winchester Model 1892 carbine.

Above Right: A German soldier during World War II checks his Luger during downtime in the fighting.

Right: A sergeant takes practice aim with a Luger; notice the natural grip angle.

Artillery Luger

The Artillery Luger featured a long 7.87-inch barrel, a tangent rear sight, and a wood shoulder stock that attached to the grip back strap. During World War I it was fitted with a 32-round drum magazine and issued to artillery troops.

Right: German artillerymen in World War I pose with their long-barrel Artillery Lugers and snail-shaped drum magazines that held 32 rounds.

.45-Caliber Luger

When the US Army was looking for a new sidearm in 1907, DWM provided test samples of Lugers chambered in .45 ACP. Of the two pistols submitted, the location of one is unknown and the other is in a private collection. Their value is estimated at about one million dollars. Mike Krause in California makes a reproduction for substantially less.

Right: The Mike Krause reproduction Luger is chambered in .45 ACP.

Browning Auto-5

The Humpback
Produced: 1903–1998

Not the most flattering nickname—Humpback—for the first successful mass-produced semiautomatic shotgun, yet it is apt, since the receiver comes straight back from the barrel and comes to a sudden stop. Unlike more modern semiautomatic shotgun receivers that gently taper into the stock, this Humpback extends the sight plane closer to the shooter's eye for fast shooting on clay pigeons or birds. I have fond memories of pheasant and grouse hunting with a "Sweet Sixteen" Auto-5 chambered in 16-gauge. The felt recoil from this shotgun is unique, more of a clunking, piston-like shove than a kick, due to the long-recoil operating system.

When a shell is fired, both the barrel and bolt move rearward. The empty shell is spit out of the ejection port and the large recoil spring drives the barrel and bolt forward, picks up a fresh shell and chambers it. It works like an industrial machine blowing all burned powder out the barrel. There is no burning gas residue buildup like in gas-operated shotguns such as the Remington 1100, Beretta AL391, and others. The Auto-5 is loaded via a port under the receiver and into a tubular magazine hidden by the forend. The magazine typically holds four rounds with one in the chamber, hence the Auto-5 name. Unique to the Browning/FN manufacture was a magazine cutoff that allowed a hunter to stop the flow of shells from the magazine and load a different round—a particularly handy feature when hunting birds and a buck walks into the scene. Flip the magazine cut off, unload the shot shell, replace with a slug, and pray the buck hasn't seen you. A system of friction rings located under the forearm and around the magazine tube regulates the recoil movement. When shooting light target loads, the rings are positioned one way; you switch them when shooting high velocity duck loads. In the old days when shot shells were made with paper hulls and swelled when wet, the Auto-5 chomped through even swelled hulls without a hitch, making it popular with duck hunters.

The Auto-5 was actually designed in 1898 by John Browning, who thought it was his "best achievement." When Winchester refused his terms on a deal, Browning brought the gun to Remington, but the then-president

Specifications
GAUGE: 20, 16, or 12
BARREL LENGTH: 26 to 32 inches
WEIGHT: 6.88 to 8 pounds (depending on barrel length/gauge)
STOCK: Checkered walnut
SIGHTS: Brass bead front, metal bead mid rib
ACTION: Long recoil-operated, semiautomatic
FINISH: Blued
CAPACITY: 4+1

Top: Chambered in 20- or 16-gauge the Auto-5 made a nice carrying and fast shooting field gun.

Right: Browning guns have always had a prestigious appeal, which this 1947 ad reinforces.

of Remington had a heart attack, killing the deal. Browning turned to FN in Belgium to manufacture the shotgun starting in 1902. Browning then licensed the design to Remington in 1905 as the Model 11, making it the first semiautomatic shotgun manufactured in the United States. Remington produced the Model 11 until 1948. The design was also licensed to Savage for their model 720, produced from 1930–1949, and other subsequent models. Browning the company ceased production in 1998, and at the time, the Auto-5 was ranked the second best selling semiautomatic shotgun in the United States just behind the Remington Model 1100.

Humpback Reborn

In 2012 Browning introduced the A5 shotgun, which looks very similar to the Auto-5 except the A5 uses what Browning calls a Kinematic Drive operating mechanism, not the original long-recoil system. The new A5 uses kinetic energy to operate the gun similar to the Inertia Drive system Benelli uses in their semiautomatic shotguns.

Below: Browning revived the Humpback look in the A5 shotgun, but the operating mechanism is different than that of the Auto-5.

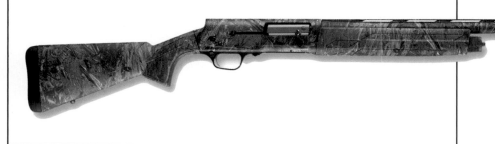

Colt M1911A1

America's Combat Pistol
Produced: 1911–Present

John Browning stood by as the United States Army put the Colt pistol, which was Browning's design, through its paces in an endurance test in 1910. The Colt pistol had six thousand rounds fired through it over the course of two days, and as the pistol heated up from the extended firing, it was simply dunked into water to cool it off. It performed flawlessly. No other pistol in the testing trials could compete against the Colt. It was a workhorse in a hard-hitting caliber that could take whatever abuse the military could throw at it. Soon after the trials, the government adopted the new Colt semiautomatic pistol in .45 ACP as the M1911. The pistol/caliber combination is as much a powerful and effective combat pistol as it is a symbol of America's power.

The M1911, and later the revised M1911A1, is our military's longest serving sidearm, and the .45 ACP cartridge is one of America's favorite rounds. The pistol has been in service with the military since 1911—hence the model designation—and today all 1911-type pistols are commonly referred to as 1911s. Though Colt was the original manufacturer and still catalogues the 1911 as the Model O, numerous firearm manufacturers produce a large variety of 1911 pistols suited for combat, law enforcement, personal defense, and competitive shooting like 3-Gun, IDPA, USPSA, and Bullseye. There are times we may wonder what we used before the 1911.

At the turn of the twentieth century during the Philippine–American War, US troops fighting Moro guerrillas found the standard issue Colt double-action revolver with swing-out cylinder chambered in .38 Long Colt an anemic weapon. The year was 1902 and the Colt revolver at the time was a high-tech weapon in the latest, greatest caliber. It took two wars for the United States government to realize the ballistic deficiency of the .38 Long Colt cartridge. The boots on the ground had a shorter learning curve. Numerous accounts told of enemy combatants being shot numerous times in vital areas with the .38 Long Colt only to keep fighting. The military's quick-fix solution was to take the Colt Single Action Army (SAA) revolver in .45 Long Colt out of mothballs. The government had

Springfield Armory in Massachusetts and the Colt factory in Connecticut rework over 16,000 Colt SAA Cavalry revolvers. These reworked revolvers would become known as Artillery models, since the refurbished guns were issued to artillery troops. America was beginning to fall in love with as well as rely on the stopping power of .45-caliber cartridges. The SAAs were a stopgap solution, but the military still needed a new service sidearm. Semiautomatic pistols were the future.

The Thompson-LaGarde Tests in 1904 tested multiple calibers—.30 Luger, 9mm, .38 Long Colt, .38 ACP, .45 Long Colt, .476 Eley, and .455 Webley—to determine the optimum bullet type and velocity for stopping effect. Five live head of cattle at the Nelson Morris Company Union stockyards and human cadavers were used in the tests. The cadavers were suspended in the air and used to measure the sway and movement of the body as it was hit with different calibers from varying distances. The wounds created in the cattle and human bodies were examined in detail and the tests confirmed a .45-caliber handgun round was optimal at providing the best shock and stopping effect. Now the only problem the US Army had was finding the right pistol and caliber combination.

Colt felt its Model 1905 pistol in .45 ACP was a suitable candidate for the new military pistol. Colt modified about two hundred Model 1905 pistols to US Military specifications and submitted them in 1907 for testing. The design needed work so John Browning went back to the drawing board, as it is said, and came up with the Model 1911 pistol. It was designed and built from the onset for combat. There was nothing subtle about the pistol. It was built to take the abuse of combat and after testing left no doubt about the Model 1911's durability, accuracy and reliability. Therefore, the Army adopted the Colt-made, Browning-designed pistol as the Automatic Pistol, Caliber .45, M1911.

Below: The Model 1907 Contract .45 was a variation of the Colt Model 1905 produced to US Military specs and the precursor to the Model 1911. Courtesy Springfield Armory National Historic Site.

The M1911 is a good place to start out when describing the 1911 platform pistol, since the basic design has not changed that much over one hundred years. The M1911 is a single-action, semiautomatic pistol that uses a recoil-operated mechanism. The original caliber for the pistol and the caliber most associated with the pistol is the .45 ACP, though numerous calibers have been chambered in the pistol since. The military .45 ACP cartridge was loaded with a 230-grain US Army Ball FMJ bullet with a muzzle velocity of 830 fps and muzzle energy of 352 ft-lbs. By today's standards the big bullet is slow moving but effective. Compared to the mil-spec M882 9mm ball ammo used by the US Military today, the 9mm round fires a 112-grain FMJ bullet at about 1263 fps. The short-recoil action designed by John Browning was nothing less than revolutionary at the time. As the round is fired both the slide and barrel recoil together for a short distance before they unlock and separate. The barrel stops its rearward motion and uses a swinging link to slightly tilt upward. At the same time the slide continues rearward, compressing the recoil spring, extracting and then ejecting the empty case, and as the recoil spring expands to change the direction of the slide, the slide feeds a fresh round from the top of the box magazine, and continues forward and finally again locks back up with the barrel. This type of short-recoil mechanism, in one form or another, has been used by nearly all pistol manufacturers ever since, making it the most common mechanism used in semiautomatic handguns in the twentieth and twenty-first centuries. Glock, SIG Sauer, CZ, HS2000/Springfield Armory XD, Smith & Wesson, Ruger, Heckler & Koch, and others all use a modified version of the short-recoil system and thus share Browning design DNA.

The M1911 feeds the fat .45 ACP cartridges from a single stack, seven-round capacity magazine, though today eight-round magazines are more common in the 1911 platform. Two automatic safety devices are utilized in the M1911. The first is a disconnector that prevents the release of the hammer unless the slide and barrel are fully forward and locked in battery. The second is a grip safety that locks the trigger unless the grip safety is pressed; grasping the gun in the firing position disengages the grip safety. A manually operated thumb safety is also built into the design. With the thumb safety engaged, both the slide and the hammer are locked in position. Original M1911s featured a long trigger and a flat main spring housing with a built-in lanyard loop. The sights consisted of a small front blade and notched rear sight set in a dovetail. Grips were checkered walnut with a double diamond pattern. Field stripping the M1911 for maintenance was simplified with the 1911 compared to other military service pistols at the time made by DWM, Bergmann, Steyr, Mauser, and others.

With tension high on the Mexico–United States border, General John J. "Black Jack" Pershing chased Pancho Villa in 1913. Some of Pershing's troops were equipped with the new M1911 pistols. The real test of the M1911, however, came the next year when the United States entered World War I. During World War I, it was found that soldiers were firing the M1911 low, so a few design modifications were made to make the M1911 easier and more comfortable to shoot accurately. An arched mainspring housing replaced the flat one which rotated the pistol higher in the operator's hand so shot would hit higher. A shorter trigger was swapped out for the longer one and the wood grips were replaced with checkered brown plastic. Material behind the trigger area on both sides of the receiver was removed to make the pistol more comfortable for the trigger finger of either a left- or right-handed shooter. The pistol also featured a parkerized finish. The modified pistol was designated the M1911A1 and manufactured prior to and during World War II.

About 1.9 million 1911A1s were built during World War II by several manufacturers including Colt, Remington Rand, Union Switch & Signal, Ithaca Gun Company, and Singer. The pistols were durable and easily refurbished to extend their service life. A testament to the M1911A1 design is its longevity and the ability to be rebuilt and reissued. No new 1911s were purchased by the government post-war. All the 1911 pistols used afterward were World War II vintage or older. The M1911A1 was used again during the Korean War, the Vietnam War, Desert Storm, and all other conflicts up to the present day with special

forces operators, even though the M1911A1 was officially replaced with the Beretta 92FS in 1985, which the US Military designated the M9. The service life of a M1911A1 is approximately 250,000 rounds; the M9 has a service life of about 25,000 rounds. The US Marine Corps was loathe to replace the 1911 and thus used remaining inventory—you can only rebuild these old warhorses so many times.

The 1911 can generally be placed into two configuration types: the Series 70 and Series 80. Original M1911s use a Series 70 configuration, in which a heavy firing pin spring prevents the firing pin from accidentally hitting the primer of a cartridge. Series 80 pistols employ a firing pin block system that requires the trigger to be fully pressed to allow the firing pin to hit the cartridge primer.

In 2012 the US Marine Corps purchased twelve thousand new 1911s, designated the M45A1 CQBP (Close Quarters Battle Pistol). The M45A1 and the M1911A1 come from the same bloodline, but the new M45A1 has modern features. A long trigger, flat main spring housing with lanyard, dual recoil spring assembly to soften recoil, a Picatinny rail for mounting accessories, a lowered and flared ejection port, large 3-dot night sights, forward slide serrations, beavertail grip safety, G10 grips, and a tan Cerakote finish are just a few of the enhancements. The M45A1 still starts like all Colt 1911s from three forgings: slide, receiver, and slide stop.

The US Military were not the only armed forces to use the 1911. Numerous other nations have used the 1911. From a law enforcement perspective, some SWAT teams favor the 1911. The LAPD SWAT team uses 1911s built by Kimber. The FBI Hostage Rescue Team and SWAT teams use 1911s. Bullseye shooters found the 1911 an easy pistol to make more accurate by using tighter slide to receiver and barrel to bushing tolerances and polished feed ramps, to name just a few tweaks. The 1911 trigger is also well suited for modifications that produce a clean crisp break with a light press. Colt began producing target 1911s in the late 1950s called Gold Cup National Match, and bullseye competition was dominated by the 1911 pistol.

Since the 1980s many manufacturers have and continue to build 1911-style pistols. Custom 1911 builders like Wilson Combat, Les Bauer, Ed Brown, Double Star, and Nighthawk Custom are just a few of the custom gun builders that have transformed the 1911 design, making the platform extremely reliable, accurate, and effective. STI International, Para USA, as well as others, have modified the 1911 to accept double stack magazines, doubling the round capacity of the pistol for use in steel plate competitions where fast shooting and plenty of ammo capacity win matches.

Today's 1911s are highly refined and purpose-built for various scenarios: concealability for personal defense, target/action shooting, and LE/military applications. They are versatile and field-proven performers that are extremely popular with civilian and LE/military users. Many modern semiautomatic pistols manufactured today owe John Browning a nod of respect for his groundbreaking design.

Gen. Keys and the M45A1 CQBP

In 2012 when the M45A1 was introduced, I had the opportunity and pleasure to speak with Lieutenant General William M. Keys about his life, his work at Colt, and especially the 1911. When you meet General Keys you have an immediate sense of wanting to please him. He fills the room with his presence and that is a feat considering we were in the boardroom of Colt Defense with a portrait of Samuel Colt. His hand is meaty and strong as we shake. My gut tells me he is stern and fair. I've read his call name in Operation Desert Storm was "Pit Bull" for good reason. I discovered he is fair and above all, he is a leader who values loyalty.

When the General uses the word "combat" he uses it as only a person who has direct experience can. In 1967 he was a young captain in the thick of it in Vietnam. In the Cam Lo district in early March 1967 Keys engaged and repelled a large enemy force. He received the Navy Cross and the Silver Star. He is humble and talks about the bonds men form when they are in combat. The 1911 is the type of pistol that also has a bond with those in combat.

After retiring from the military, Keys found himself on Wall Street and took the job of president and CEO of Colt. He has since retired as CEO and now sits on the board of directors. Keys readily admits he was not trained as a businessman, but he knew how to lead, and he is credited with getting Colt back in the game. He believes quality is important, and nothing leaves the factory if it is not the best Colt can build.

"The 1911 is an old design, and a design that works," said Lt. Gen. Keys. "The Marines, in fact all the branches of the US Military, have carried the 1911 for over one hundred years, and naturally the Marines took a look at the 1911 again. The 1911 is a gun that is designed to shoot and kill. And it does that. Using the gun in combat is a whole different experience than shooting tin cans. There are a lot who think they know the gun, but they don't. The gun in combat is part of you. You bond with it as much as you do the guys you fight with. Once you become familiar with it, it is accurate and dependable. John Browning was a pretty sharp guy. When you pull this pistol from your holster it fits your, points naturally, and in combat you are shooting close and fast."

The difference between the M45A1 and the last 1911 that was used by the US Military, the 1911A1, is like night and day. "The M45A1 is a souped-up version of the 1911A1," explained the General. "It is based on the Rail Gun, which Colt has been making for years, and the M45A1 is an enhanced version of the Rail Gun." Externally the

Below: The similarities between the M45A1 prototype and Colt Rail production gun are close.

M45A1 is similar to the Rail Gun, but internally it is better. It has a stainless national match barrel, better trigger, and dual recoil spring like those used in the Colt Delta Elite for a softer recoil. "There is a great clamoring for the 1911 to come back as a service weapon all across the military because of its reliability, knock-down power, ease to shoot," added the General. With other polymer-framed striker-fired pistols on the market as well as other manufacturers building 1911 pistols, it is a bit of poetic justice that Colt and the 1911 were awarded the contract by the Marines.

Above: Author test firing the M45A1 at a Colt test range in Farmington, Connecticut.

Commanders and Officers

Common 1911 variants produced by Colt include the Commander, which features a 4.25-inch barrel and full-size receiver. The Commander was first produced starting in 1950 and was the first mass-produced pistol with an aluminum frame. It was also the first Colt pistol to be chambered in 9mm. The Officer models were introduced in 1985 and offered .45 ACP stopping power in a smaller compact version with a 3.5-inch barrel. Smaller variants of the 1911 design are offered by a variety of other manufacturers, with Kimber producing a Pro model with a 4-inch barrel and full size frame, a Compact variant with a short grip frame and 4-inch barrel, an Ultra+ with a 3-inch barrel and full length frame, and an Ultra with 3-inch barrel and short grip frame.

Specifications

CALIBER: 9mm, .38 Super, .40 S&W, .45 ACP (most common)

BARREL LENGTH: 5.0 in.

OA LENGTH: 8.3 in.

WEIGHT: 37.0 oz. (unloaded)

ACTION: recoil-operated, autoloader, single-action

CAPACITY: 7 + 1 (.45 ACP)

Right: The Les Baer Premier II is an example of a popular custom 1911 based off the 5-inch barrel full-size government model and is suitable for duty, defense, or competition. The accuracy guarantee is 3-inch groups at 50 yards. Courtesy Les Baer.

Below: The Kimber Ultra CDP II is a compact 1911 variant with a 3-inch barrel, short grip frame, and a 7+1 capacity.

Winchester Model 12

Perfect Pump
Produced: 1912–1975, 1993–1995 (Winchester), 1988–1992 (Browning)

There are pump shotguns and then there is the Winchester Model 12, the slickest cycling easiest pointing pump shotgun that was ever built. You can shoot the Model 12 until the bluing wears off and the Model 12 just keeps on going. All other pump shotguns, whether deserved or not, are compared to the Model 12. Advertisements read, "Everyone Shoots Better with a Model 12." In this case there was truth in advertising. Hunters and clay shooters alike dropped birds and dusted clays with an uncanny ability using the Model 12. There is a reason it was called the "Perfect Repeater."

The designer of the Model 12 was Winchester engineer T.C. Johnson. Compared to previous Winchester shotguns, and the Model 1897 in particular, the Model 12 was a departure. An internal hammer was housed in a streamlined receiver machined from forged steel. Earlier models allowed the shooter to slam fire the shotgun by holding back the trigger and pumping the action to fire. Later models changed this by adding a trigger disconnector. The safety button was located forward of the trigger guard, conveniently located where the shooter rested a finger prior to firing the gun. The Model 12 had the ability to easily interchange barrels, but there were no choke tubes in these old-school shooters. The Model 12 featured an American black walnut buttstock and forend. Shells are loaded via a port located in the bottom of the receiver and into a magazine tube. Empties are ejected to the right. Initially the Model 12 was only available in 20-gauge but by 1913 16- and 12-gauge models were coming off the assembly lines.

In the 1950s, the heyday of shotgunning, the Model 12 was offered in a variety of configurations in addition to the standard Field model. Barrels were of Winchester Proof Steel barrels in lengths of 26, 28, and 30 inches choked full, modified, and improved cylinder.

The Super Field, Pigeon Grade, Magnum Duck Gun, Skeet, and Trap competition guns featured checkered stocks with pistol grip caps and checkered forends. Guns could be offered custom fit to a shooter's dimensions, and better wood and engraving were options.

Specifications
GAUGE: 28, 20, 16, 12
BARREL LENGTH: 25, 26, 28, 30, or 32 inches
OA LENGTH: 49.5 inches (30-inch barrel)
WEIGHT: 7.4 lbs. (30-inch barrel, 12-gauge)
STOCK: Checkered American black walnut
SIGHTS: Brass bead front
ACTION: Pump-action
CHOKE: Fixed, various
FINISH: Polished blue receiver/barrel
CAPACITY: 6+1 (2-3/4-in. shells)

Top: The Winchester Model 12 is known as the Perfect Repeater due to its excellent pointability, slick operating action, and legendary reliability.

Like many items built a century ago, the Model 12 was hand-fitted. Labor was intense and so was the cost to produce these grand shotguns. Shotguns like the Remington Model 870 were offered at significantly lower prices than the Model 12. Some two million Model 12s were built by Winchester, while Browning at times has offered limited editions of the Model 12. By 1964 production at Winchester ceased.

The Model 12 was not just used by hunters and target shooters. Law enforcement and the military made use of the Model 12 as well. Riot and trench gun variants were equipped with a heat shield over the barrel and a bayonet lug. Model 12s were used during both World Wars, the Korean War, and the Vietnam War.

The Model 12 is the king of the pump guns. The Perfect Repeater indeed.

Left: In 1952 Winchester's advertisement for the Model 12 claimed: Everyone Shoots Better with a Model 12.

Opposite Page: A trait of the Model 12 was it never wore out, even over a lifetime of hard use. This advertisement drives the point home.

for a lifetime of shooting — buy a

PRICED FROM $104.95*

WINCHESTER ——— MODEL 12
TRADEMARK

Good News! Only $10.95 down and up to 20 months to pay puts the superb Model 12 in your hands. See your local Winchester Time Payment Plan dealer for details.

WINCHESTER
FIREARMS
TIME PAYMENT PLAN

*PRICES SUBJECT TO CHANGE WITHOUT NOTICE

No shotgun made anywhere in the world can take it like a Model 12! Built of better materials, to a better design, by craftsmen to whom perfection is the only standard, a Winchester Model 12 is a treasured possession often handed from father to son. For 45 years the Model 12 has been the choice of sportsmen who know the best costs the least in the long run — make the 12 *your* choice, too.

action pictures prove

— that in less than 3/5 of a second a hunter can raise and fire a superbly balanced Model 12. Speed? You bet! The kind you must have for fast, fleet game.

25 wear adjustments

Tough Winchester Proof-Steel, machined to exact dimensions gives you years of extra use before any take-up is necessary. Then you can make a slight adjustment and get years more. *No Model 12 has ever used all the adjustment available!* Tough? And how!

WINCHESTER-WESTERN DIVISION · OLIN MATHIESON CHEMICAL CORPORATION · NEW HAVEN 4, CONN.

Right: This is a Browning Model 42 Limited Edition Grade V with engraving and gold inlays. Courtesy Bishops Fine Guns.

A Mini Model 12

Instead of reengineering the Model 12 to fire the diminutive .410 shell, Winchester designed a scaled-down, reduced sized Model 42. It was Winchester's first pump shotgun designed for the .410. Like the Model 12, the Model 42 was available in different grades and was produced by Winchester from 1933 to 1963. Browning offered a limited edition of the Model 42 from 1991 to 1993.

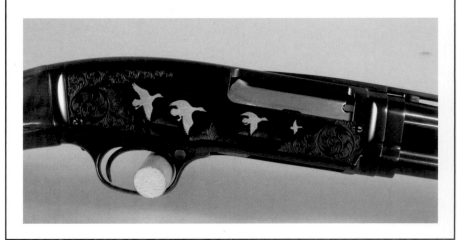

Walther PPK

The Compact Pistol That Shook, Not Stirred
Produced: 1930–Present

Pocket pistols first appeared in Walther's product line in 1908, making them one of the very first firearm companies to manufacture small, compact pistols. That DNA has always been entwined in all Walther pistols, especially in the svelte-looking PPK.

The Walther Model PPK (*Polizeipistole Kriminalmodell,* or *Police Pistol Detective Model!*) was one of Walther's early designs to successfully use steel stampings in a compact pistol. The PPK was designed for police use in 1930. It followed the introduction of the Walther PP (*Polizeipistole*), which is basically the same as the PPK but uses a longer 3.9-inch barrel and a full steel frame. The PP was introduced in 1929. Today steel stampings are common, and the PPK is iconic. The pistol is still extremely popular today with law enforcement agencies as a backup gun and civilians holding concealed carry permits. The German military used it extensively during World War II, and Ian Fleming armed his famous spy character, James Bond, with the PPK. The PPK's size, caliber, simple controls, ease of use, and the pistol's relentless reliability make it a benchmark in compact pistols. All compact pistols manufactured since owe many design characteristics to the PPK.

The compact PPK pistol uses a simple blow back operating system and features a traditional DA/SA trigger; a single stack magazine with a thin grip, a barrel fixed to the frame, exposed hammer, and decocking lever are some of the other features. Some magazines also include a floor plate with a finger rest. The checkered plastic grips of the pistol form the pistol's back strap. Old school for sure, but ever so effective. A trademark feature of the PPK is the decocking safety lever. With the hammer cocked all the way back the safety is rotated downward, decocking the hammer and allowing it to fall against the decocking lever. This model also has loaded chamber indicators that can be seen and felt in the dark if need be, telling the user a round is in the chamber. Models are available in a matte stainless steel finish or a traditional deep blue.

The PPK/S is mechanically the same as the PPK but uses a longer full metal frame that holds 7+1 rounds, of .380 ammo. PPK/S models mate a PP frame to a PPK slide to meet United States firearms importation guidelines set down

Specifications

CALIBER: .22 LR, .25 ACP, .32 ACP; .380

BARREL LENGTH: 3.3 inches

OA LENGTH: 6.1 inches

WEIGHT: 21 ounces (unloaded)

STOCK: Checkered plastic

SIGHTS: Fixed notch rear/blade front

ACTION: Straight blow back, semiautomatic

FINISH: Deep blue or stainless (later variants)

CAPACITY: 8+1 (.22 LR), 7+1 (.32 ACP), 6+1 (.380)

by the Gun Control Act of 1968. The PP, PPK, and PPK/S family of pistols are some of the most popular and successful small pistols ever designed.

During World War II the PPK was issued to numerous German military and police forces. Adolf Hitler is purported to have committed suicide with a PPK in his bunker stronghold in Berlin as the Allies and Soviets entered the city.

The PPK inspired other small pistol designs like the Soviet Makarov, Bersa Thunder 380 from Argentina, the Hungarian FEG PA-63, and more. Though smaller and lighter polymer-frame pistols have taken away market share, the PPK's influence and notoriety was sealed when Ian Fleming issued the PPK to his secret agent character, James Bond, in his series of spy novels. PPK has been licensed by Manurhin in France, and it is now licensed by Smith & Wesson. Originals were made in Zella-Mehlis, Germany.

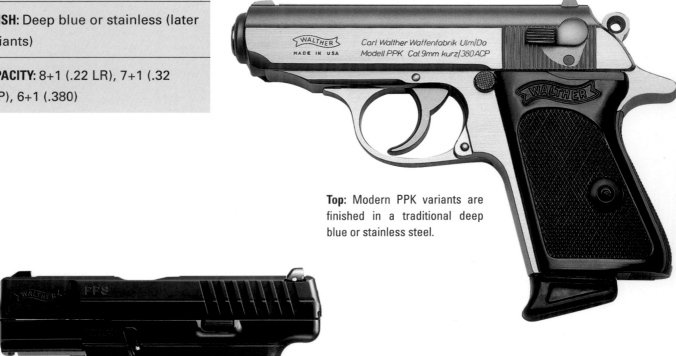

Top: Modern PPK variants are finished in a traditional deep blue or stainless steel.

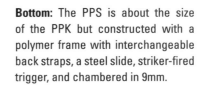

Bottom: The PPS is about the size of the PPK but constructed with a polymer frame with interchangeable back straps, a steel slide, striker-fired trigger, and chambered in 9mm.

Dr. No

Ian Fleming, the creator of the James Bond character and author of some seventeen Bond novels and short stories, was chided by British expert in firearms Geoffrey Boothroyd for Fleming's choice of firearm for Bond—originally a Beretta M418. Boothroyd suggested a Walther PPK 7.65mm and Fleming took the advice, arming Bond with the PPK in *Dr. No*. In thanks to Boothroyd, Fleming named an MI6 armorer in the book Major Boothroyd.

Modern Pocket Pistols

Manufacturers such as Kahr, Ruger, Glock, and Kel-Tec, to name a few, use high-tech polymer frames and CNC machining to elevate the pocket pistol in firepower and concealability. Modern compact and subcompact pistols are light, and some are chambered in larger calibers.

Left Top: The Kahr CT380 is chambered in .380 and weighs only 11.4 ounces unloaded.

LeftBottom: The Glock G43 is slightly over 1-inch thick and holds 6+1 rounds of 9mm ammo.

Right Top: The economical .32 ACP Kel-Tec P-32 uses a polymer frame and weighs 6.6 ounces unloaded.

Right Bottom: The Ruger LC9 has about the same dimensions as the PPK but offers 7+1 rounds of 9mm firepower.

Walther Brings Sexy Back

The PK380 is built with a polymer frame and steel slide and barrel. The first thing you will notice when you pick up the PK380 is how good the grip feels in your hand. From a petite female to hulking brute, the PK380 feels right in anyone's hand and it naturally points. A finger rest is built into the magazine floor plate so your little finger—if you have a big hand—does not dangle off the bottom of the grip. The PK380 is angular and aggressive looking. The controls consist of an ambidextrous safety mounted on the slide near the thumb of either a right- or left-handed shooter. Flip it up to fire the gun, rotate it down to put it on safe. The magazine release is also ambidextrous and built into the trigger guard so it is easy to release the magazine with whatever

hand you shoot with. The trigger is traditional DA/SA meaning the first shot is first DA (double-action) requiring more effort to press the trigger, then once the round is fired the action goes into SA (single-action) which requires a lot less effort to press the trigger. The Walther PK380 is a provocative and inviting compact pistol. I found myself picking up the pistol often. In hand, it feels sensuous and fits my hand nearly perfectly.

Top: There is not a lot of ramp-up time required to start shooting the PK380 well.

Bottom: While other pistol manufacturers have gone the micro design route, building .380 pistols that are small and ultra concealable, the PK380 is slightly larger though still very compact.

Mauser Karabiner 98 Kurz

Last Great Bolt-Action Battle Rifle
Produced: 1935–1945

The Mauser name and company has been synonymous with control-feed bolt-action rifles since 1870. Militaries around the world found Mauser rifles to be a tremendous asset in any conflict—reliable, fast to reload, and durable. Mauser rifles equipped armies in Europe, South America, the Middle East, and Asia from the late nineteenth century through the twentieth century.

The Mauser Karabiner 98k, also referred to as K98, Kar98k, or K98k, was the consummate and final bolt-action battle rifle and the standard issue service rifle adopted in 1935 by the German *Wehrmacht* prior to World War II. Over fourteen million were produced, and there are still countless numbers still being used to protect homes, to hunt, or to incite revolution.

Based on the Mauser M98 rifle, the K98k is a shorter, carbine model. It uses a control feed bolt-action with three locking lugs that have a 90-degree bolt lift. The bolt cocks on opening. The bolt knob is larger than that of a hunting rifle and the wood stock is inlet to allow quick access. The three-position safety is classic Mauser. The lever, when viewed from the rear, clearly indicates to the operator the state of the weapon. Full left and weapon is ready to fire. Vertical position blocks the sights and tells the user the rifle is on safe but the bolt is unlocked and can be operated to reload the rifle. To the right and the rifle is on safe and the bolt is locked and cannot be operated. To remove the bolt, put the safety lever in the vertical position and open the bolt and pull it back. On the left side and to the rear of the receiver is the bolt stop release lever. It is hinged, swinging from the front to rear, and spring loaded. Pull the forward section of the bolt stop away from the receiver and hold it outward, then remove the bolt from the receiver.

The K98k uses an internal box magazine loaded with a five-round stripper clip. The bolt is fully opened to the rear and the stripper clip is inserted into the rear notches of the receiver. The cartridges are then pushed down using your thumb. The stripper clip can then be removed by hand or it will be pushed out of the rifle as the bolt is closed and round chambered.

Specifications:

CALIBER: 7.92x57mm, also known as 8mm Mauser or 8x57mm

BARREL LENGTH: 24.2 inches

OA LENGTH: 43.7 in.

WEIGHT: 8.2 lb. (unloaded)

STOCK: Oil-resistant laminated wood

SIGHTS: Adjustable rear/hooded post front or 1.5x ZF-41 long eye relief riflescope

ACTION: Bolt, control feed, two-lug

FINISH: Blued

CAPACITY: 5+1

During World War II numerous arms factories produced the K98k—Mauser, Sauer, Erma, and others. The rifles are coded so if you come across a K98k, you can identify the manufacturer and date produced. Rifles with Nazi SS markings are extremely valuable now. Optics may seem like a relatively modern feature for a combat rifle, but a variant of the 98k was equipped with 1.5x power scope and designated the 98k-ZF 41. Nearly ninety thousand 98k-ZF 41s were sent to the field and there they served as a sharpshooter's weapon, not a true sniper weapon. The optic did give the operator an edge just like the Trijicon and Eclan optics, as well as others, do today.

Commercially the M98 was produced from 1898 through 1946. If you were going on a hunt to Africa, the Mauser was the rifle to carry. Since they use a control round feed these rifles were well suited for hunting dangerous game that could stomp a hunter to a gooey pulp.

Today Mauser is still producing the M98 and if your budget allows, you can purchase a rifle storied in war as well as the hunting field.

Top: A stripper clip is used to quickly load the Mauser, or cartridges can be loaded one at a time.

Middle: The K98 in use during World War II—the rifle was well balanced and fired the powerful 7.92x57mm Mauser cartridge.

Bottom: The German *Wehrmacht* configured a number of 98k with a low-power scope designating the 98k-ZF 41 for use as a sharpshooter's or designated rifleman's weapon.

Mauser Knock-Off

After the brief Spanish-American War, the US Army analyzed captured 1893 Spanish Mausers. The Mauser's edge over the Krag rifle during the conflict was apparent. In 1900 a design was finalized by the US Army that borrowed many Mauser design features—fixed internal magazine, dual forward lug bolt, bolt-mounted safety, and magazine cut-off. An effort was made by the US Military to make the new design, named the M1903, different from the Mauser with a two-piece firing pin and third safety lug, among other details. Production began on the Springfield 1903 at the federal armory in Springfield, Massachusetts. When Mauser became aware of the M1903, it filed a patent infringement suit in United States courts and won.

Below: Here US troops proudly display their M1903s; the rifle was well liked by soldiers due to its accuracy and reliability.

The Legend Lives

The M98 rifle was so durable and accurate it was not long before it was sporterized and turned into a hunting rifle. Mauser currently offers the M98 in standard and magnum caliber configurations. The Mauser is legendary with hunters across Europe, in Africa, and near anywhere big game is hunted.

Top: These are current manufacture M98 rifles, legendary for their workmanship and performance in the field.

Bottom: Though manufactured in the twenty-first century, this M98 still used the Mauser three-position safety and side bolt release lever.

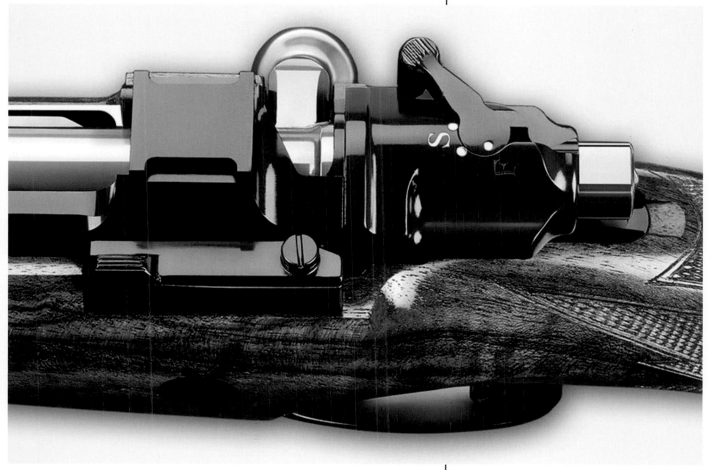

M1 Garand

The Greatest Generation's Combat Rifle
Produced: 1936–1957, early 1980s

With a full moon and a high tide Allied naval guns belched hellfire in the dawn of June 6, 1944. The bombardment pummeled the beaches—Utah, Omaha, Gold, Juno, and Sword—from the sea. Army troops soon climbed down the sides of ships into landing craft, vehicle, personnel (LCVP). The Allied landings in Normandy had begun. In the LCVPs it was all helmets and M1 muzzles, some covered with prophylactics. They were told the condoms would protect the bore from salt water. Enemy artillery missed, punching holes in the water and drenching troops. Some puked on their boots; it was their second boat ride. German machine gun bullets pecked at the steel sides of LCVPs as they plowed closer to the beach. Then the LCVPs stopped and all at once the ramps dropped.

The Greatest Generation was birthed from those landing crafts onto the beaches of D-Day in blood, sand, and seawater, changing the course of World War II in Europe. At every step of the way was the M1 Garand rifle, officially called the United States Rifle, Caliber .30, or more commonly the M1. The M1 was revolutionary. It was America's first semiautomatic battle rifle and easily outclassed Germany's and Japan's manually operated bolt-action rifles. Eight shots could be fired as quickly as the trigger was pressed. With a rate of fire of forty to fifty rounds per minute, the M1 offered superior firepower over the slower firing five-shot German Mauser K98 and the five-shot Japanese Arisaka Type 99 rifle. Army Chief of Staff General Douglas MacArthur said the "Garand rifle is one of the greatest contributions to our

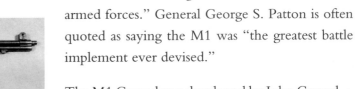

armed forces." General George S. Patton is often quoted as saying the M1 was "the greatest battle implement ever devised."

The M1 Garand was developed by John Garand—pronounced like "errand"—who was born in Saint-Rémi, Quebec, Canada, in 1888, and as a child moved with his family to Jewett City, Connecticut. Textile mills were quite common in New England at that time and Garand, still a

teen, became employed at one of the mills working his way up to machinist. Garand showed great aptitude for machinery. He also liked guns. In 1917 the US Army solicited designs on a lightweight machine gun. Garand submitted a design that was accepted. From that point on he was hired by the government, first to fine-tune his machine gun design at the Springfield Armory in Springfield, Massachusetts, and then eventually he was assigned the task of designing a semiautomatic rifle for infantry use. After about fifteen years of design and development, Garand began manufacturing his design in 1928 and patented the M1 in 1934.

The M1's operating system uses a gas-operated, long-stroke piston. The AK-47 uses a similar system. The one-piece operating rod consists of the long-stroke piston and an operating rod handle. The rotating bolt features two locking lugs on its face. Originally the M1 featured a gas trap in a muzzle extension. This set-up was complicated and the design was revised in 1940 to use a gas port drilled in the bottom of the barrel. The rifle's mechanism is cycled when expanding gases from a fired cartridge travel through the port and into a gas cylinder holding the long stroke piston. The gas pushes the piston and operating rod rearward to unlock the rotating bolt housed in the receiver. As the bolt travels rearward it ejects an empty case then reverses direction and moves forward scraping a fresh round out of the M1. The M1 was designed to be simple to disassemble and assemble. It takes seconds to field strip an M1 into three main groups: barrel and receiver, buttstock, and trigger. Parts easily snap together. The M1 began to set the standard for future combat rifles.

Part of the M1's enduring legacy is its cartridge. Originally the rifle design was chambered in .276 Pedersen, an experimental 7mm round the military was developing. General MacArthur nixed the idea of the experimental round and the M1 design was converted to use the .30-06 Springfield cartridge, for which there were stockpiles of ammunition on hand. The predecessors of the M1 Garand, the bolt-action 1903 Springfield and M1917 Enfield rifles, were chambered in .30-06. The .30-06 Springfield is a benchmark caliber by which all other calibers are compared in the United States. GIs returning home from World War I, who had used the '06 in Enfields, soon brought the round to deer camp and when the Great Generation returned to deer camp the .30-06 Springfield would soon be entrenched as America's favorite hunting cartridge.

The Garand rifle used a smart, high tech feature of the day—an en-bloc clip that held eight cartridges—allowing an operator to quickly load the M1 by locking back the operating handle and pushing the clip into the M1's internal magazine. It was fast and efficient. Surprisingly, at the time the US Military thought detachable box magazines like those found on the M1's contemporary, the British Lee-Enfield rifle, were less reliable and prone to loss and accumulated debris in the magazine well. This view changed when the US Military adopted the M1 Carbine. Upon firing the last round in the M1, the clip was ejected with a characteristic metallic pinging sound. A myth behind the M1's "ping" is that enemy soldiers waited for the sound of the ping and took advantage of GIs reloading their M1s. After the war, interviews with both Japanese and German combatants found the sound of the ping couldn't be heard over the clamor of a firefight.

The iron sights of the M1 were exceedingly sturdy and well suited for battle. In fact current mil-spec AR15 sights are similar to sights used on the M1. The safety was also pure common sense. A steel tab located in the front of the trigger guard is rotated toward the trigger and inside the trigger. An operator can easily tell if the rifle has the safety engaged with a finger in the trigger guard. Manual safety mechanism designs like this have since been deemed less safe than other designs because the operator's finger is inside the trigger guard, creating the potential for an accidental discharge. Regardless, the M14, which replaced the M1, and the Ruger Mini-14 and Mini-Thirty are examples of rifle designs since the M1 that use a similar manual safety system.

The M1 Garand was revolutionary, if not radical, at the time it was adopted as the standard issue rifle for the US Military in 1936. Though adopted, the rifle went through a number of design and production tweaks before rolling off Winchester and Springfield Armory production lines. At its production peak, six hundred rifles were manufactured a day. By 1941 the Army was fully equipped with new M1s. Some 3.8 million rifles were built with production ceasing in 1945.

Numerous variants on the M1 were built. Some experimental models were made with shorter barrels, detachable magazines, and other features thought to be useful to the modern combat soldier. Sniper variants—the M1C and M1D—were built by the end of World War II, but they saw limited use. Since the clip was inserted and ejected out of the top of the receiver, optics were side mounted to the M1s. M1Cs and M1Ds used either 2.5x power M81/M82 or 2.2x power M84 scopes and a leather cheek pad. M1Ds also had an M2 flash suppressor. During the Korean War American snipers maintained

Specifications

CALIBER: .30-06 Springfield (7.62x63mm)

BARREL LENGTH: 24 inches

OA LENGTH: 43.5 inches

WEIGHT: 9.5 to 11.6 pounds

STOCK: Smooth wood (various types)

SIGHTS: Adjustable rear aperture/ winged front post

ACTION: Gas-operated long stroke piston/rotating bolt, semiautomatic

FINISH: Parkerized

CAPACITY: 8-round en-bloc clip/ internal magazine

EFFECTIVE RANGE: 500 yards

consistent accuracy out to six hundred yards with the M1 sniper variants, giving American forces an edge in some of the trench warfare.

There is little doubt of the impact the M1 Garand had on the outcome of the war. The M1 was carried to victory in World War II in both the European and Pacific theaters. After the war the rifles were shipped back to the States and refurbished. As the Korean War unfolded in June of 1950, GIs were equipped with the venerable albeit rebuilt post-WWII M1s. The War Department, however, foresaw the need for additional M1s and contracted with International Harvester and Harrington & Richardson in the early 1950s to produce more Garands. Including World War II production, the total number of M1 Garands built was about 6.25 million. Overseas the M1 was built by Breda and Beretta. By the time the Vietnam War had begun, the M1 was still being called to duty and issued to reserve troops into the early 1970s, although it had been officially replaced in 1957 as a frontline-service weapon with the M14.

Into the 1980s, the Garand was still in use by some militaries of numerous countries. During its reign as a premier battle rifle, the M1 was used by Greece, Denmark, Jordan, Republic of Korea, Norway, and South Vietnam, among others. Today the M1 Garand is still used by the US Marine Corps Silent Drill Team and the US Air Force Academy Cadet Honor Guard as well as ROTC teams and some foreign military drill teams. Civilians by far are the biggest users of the M1 Garand today. The Civilian Marksman Program (CMP) allows qualified individuals to purchase surplus M1s. The M1 is used in Service Rifles matches across the country where it is fired from a variety of shooting positions—standing, kneeling, sitting, and prone—at targets from two hundred yards out to six hundred yards. Others collect Garands. Garand collectors prize a gas trap M1, as most gas trap models were retrofitted to the gas port design. Some have used the M1 for hunting but the M1's heft—on average ten pounds—make it a heavy rifle to tote as well as not being easy to mount a scope.

The M1 Garand proved its battle worthiness as an accurate and durable rifle in a variety of severe environmental conditions during World War II—sand and seawater on the beaches during D-Day, intense cold during the Battle of the Bulge, and the heat and humidity of jungles in the Pacific Theater in places like Iwo Jima, Guadalcanal, Okinawa, and elsewhere. Today the M1 Garand is prized as a classic military rifle still capable of shooting the black out of bull's-eyes in competition.

Garand Thumb

Incorrect handling causes an M1 Garand's bolt to slam forward onto the operator's thumb, thus causing what is called "M1 thumb" or "Garand thumb." Typically the operator has failed to fully lock the bolt rearward, and friction between the moving parts temporarily seizes the bolt. When the operator pushes down on the follower or accidentally bumps the rifle, the bolt slams forward. A stream of expletives typically follows an occurrence of Garand Thumb.

Clips: Stripper, Moon, Half Moon, and En-Bloc

A clip is a device that holds multiple rounds of ammunition as one unit so it can be quickly inserted into a firearm's internal magazine. The Springfield 1903A3, SKS rifles, and Mauser 1896 pistol use a stripper clip that keeps cartridges in a single column. The stripper is inserted into the magazine and the operator presses down on the cartridges stripping them from the clip and into the weapon's magazine. The stripper clip is then tossed. The M1917 and S&W M625 are two examples of revolvers that use half-moon and moon clips. Half-moon clips hold three rounds; moon clips hold six rounds. The clips allow the revolver's chambers to be loaded more quickly than if each round were loading separately. The M1 Garand uses an en-bloc clip that holds a double stack column of eight cartridges. Both the en-bloc clip and cartridges are loaded into the M1's magazine. After the last round is fired the en-bloc clip is ejected from the magazine. Want to annoy a Garand collector? Call a magazine a clip or a clip a magazine. Do so at your own risk.

Winchester Model 70

Specifications

CALIBER: .22 Hornet, .222 Remington, .223 Remington, .22-250 Remington, .223 WSSM, .225 Winchester, .220 Swift, .243 Winchester, .243 WSSM, .250-3000 Savage, .257 Roberts, .25-06 Remington, .25 WSSM, 6.5x55mm, .264 Winchester Magnum, .270 Winchester, .270 WSM, .270 Weatherby Magnum, 280 Rem., 7mm Mauser, 7mm-08, 7 mm Remington Magnum, 7mm WSM, 7mm STW, .300 Savage, .30-06 Springfield, .308 Winchester, .300 H&H Magnum, .300 Winchester Magnum, .300 WSM, .300 Weatherby Magnum, .300 RUM, .325 WSM, .338 Winchester Magnum, .35 Remington, .358 Winchester, .375 H&H Magnum, .416 Remington Magnum, .416 Rigby, .458 Winchester Magnum, .470 Capstick

BARREL LENGTH: 20, 22, or 24 in. (depending on caliber/model)

WEIGHT: 6.75 to 7.25 lb. (depending on caliber)

STOCK: Checkered wood (standard)

The Rifleman's Rifle—Really
Produced: 1936–1963 (pre-'64), 1964–1994 (push feed), 1994–Present (Classic)

If there ever was an iconic bolt-action hunting rifle, it is the Winchester Model 70. Of course it really depends on when the Model 70 was manufactured. Collectors and hunters group the rifle into three manufacturing periods. The first is Pre '64 rifles, which are the most desirable—the sweet spot of Model 70 manufacturing—and were built between 1936 and 1963. These rifles use a Mauser-style control round feed system with a two-lug bolt with 90-degree lift, three-position safety, blade type ejector, a cone-shaped breech that funnels cartridges into the chamber, a machined steel floor plate, and excellent trigger, among other features. It was the type of rifle hunters aspired to own. These rifles made the Model 70 legendary.

The next period in the Model 70 evolution was the push feed models built from 1964 to 1994, which was an attempt to make the Model 70 more economical to manufacture. These rifles were slightly more accurate than the Pre-'64 models, but they were ugly and to Winchester purists it rubbed their fur the wrong way. These rifles used a push-feed system in lieu of the controlled-feed system and gave Winchester a black eye while turning off many Winchester enthusiasts.

The third period of manufacture is considered the Classic and began in 1994 when Winchester finally wised up and reverted back to the Pre '64 control feed style action. These current models have redeemed the iconic rifle maker back to the status it had when Pre '64 rifles were the darling rifle of gun writers like Jack O'Connor, killed dangerous beasts in Africa, and won target shooting competitions.

Winchester's experience with bolt-action rifles took hold with the hunting public beginning in 1925 with the introduction of the Model 54, which was the first successful commercial bolt-action rifle Winchester produced. The Model 54 was a fine rifle but expensive to manufacture, hard to mount an optic (which was becoming the norm with hunters in those days), as well as some other design features that needed tweaking. Winchester set its engineers onto the task and the result was the Model 70, which began rolling off the assembly line in 1936. Rifles could be had in grades starting from Standard; Featherweight was a light-weight variant with a specific checkering style on the stock and a scannable forearm; Super Grade with fancy walnut, ebony forearm tip, and jeweled bolt; Super Grade Featherweight; Super Grade African with express iron sights and chambered in big bore calibers; a Varmint grade with a heavy 26-inch barrel; and Alaskan grade. Competition models included a National Match, Target, and Bull Gun all with heavy, stout barrels. A carbine variant with a 20-inch barrel was also offered between 1936 and 1946 though Winchester never officially used the "carbine" nomenclature. The Model 70 was advertised as the "rifleman's rifle" and that name took. Chambered in calibers that range from the puny .22 Hornet to the mighty .458 Winchester Magnum, the Model 70 plied its trade on gopher- to pachyderm-sized game.

During World War II the Marines were in need of a sniper rifle and used Model 70 rifles they had intended for training. Combat and environment are hard on rifles and the Model 70 was reconditioned with different stocks to better perform. When the Marines began looking at a dedicated sniper rifle, which would become the M40, they deep sixed the Model 70 as the push feed model was then being built. The Marines opted to start the build using a Remington Model 700 action.

The Model 70 was produced in New Haven, Connecticut, for some seventy years with production stopping in 2006—a bad day in New Haven—but starting up again south of the Mason-Dixon line in Columbia, South Carolina, in 2008. Deer and elk hunters are just happy the Model 70 is back with control feed as originally designed.

SIGHTS: Adjustable rear/hooded brass bead front

ACTION: Bolt, control feed, two-lug

FINISH: Blued (standard) or stainless (Classic)

CAPACITY: 3+1 or 5+1 (depending on caliber)

Below: Example of an older Winchester Model 70 Super Grade with fancy walnut, ebony tip forearm, and jeweled bolt. Courtesy Bishops Fine Guns.

Top: The current Model 70 Featherweight has a distinct looking stock and offers less weight for ease in handling.

Right: An advertisement from the 1970s worked the "Rifleman's rifle" tagline.

Opposite Page: In 1952 Winchester was producing two of the most popular deer rifles of the time, the Model 70 bolt-action and Model 94 lever-action.

Jack's Rifle

Jack O'Connor hunted a Model 70 in .270 Winchester over numerous continents. O'Connor evangelized the Model 70 in the pages of *Outdoor Life* and his numerous books about his exploits with the Model 70. His stories are great hunting literature. In *The Art of Hunting Big Game in North America,* O'Conner wrote ". . . whenever I go out for the noble rams I'll take one of a matched pair of Model 70 Winchester featherweights in .270 caliber." O'Connor used a Redfield Bear Cub 4x scope on one and a Leupold 4x on the other. He could take shots out to four hundred yards with these set-ups. When O'Connor was told the Model 70 was going to be redesigned, he said he wanted to buy four or five of the older model. And when he saw the new Model 70 prototype, the push feed model, he said it was one of the ugliest rifles he had ever seen and it wouldn't sell. Winchester took some of O'Connor's suggestions and O'Connor ended up changing his mind about the rifle.

Top: Jack O'Connor and his son Brad at a successful moose hunt in British Columbia. Courtesy Jack O'Connor Hunting Heritage and Education Center; jack-oconnor.org.

Right: The old man and his sheep, O'Connor hunted sheep with a pair of Winchester Model 70s both chambered in .270 Winchester. Courtesy Jack O'Connor Hunting Heritage and Education Center; jack-oconnor.org.

Makeshift Sniper Rifle

During World War II the Marines had Model 70 rifles on hand for training but called the rifles into service in the Pacific Theater. They were also used in the Korean War. They were chambered in .30-06 with a 24-inch, hunting-style taper barrel. After Korea, many of the rifles were reconditioned with a heavier barrel and the stocks were also bedded to free float the barrel to aid accuracy. Unertl 8x power scope, the high-tech optic of the day, was typically mounted on the Model 70s. During the Vietnam War these reconditioned Model 70s were issued to snipers like legendary Marine sniper Gunnery Sergeant Carlos Hathcock. Hathcock used a Model 70 to kill a North Vietnamese sniper in a famous shot. He killed the enemy sniper by shooting him in the eye through the riflescope of the enemy sniper.

Left: Here a Marine sniper plies his trade with a Model 70 set up for sniper work.

Ithaca Model 37

Specifications

GAUGE: .410, 28, 20, 16, 12 (3-in. chamber)

BARREL LENGTH: 18.5 (trench/riot variants); 24, 26, 28 or 30 inches (commercial variants)

OA LENGTH: 47.6 inches (28-in. barrel, 12-gauge)

WEIGHT: 7.6 lbs. (28-in. barrel, 12-gauge)

STOCK: Checkered fancy black walnut (Featherweight)

SIGHTS: Tru Glo front, metal bead mid rib (Featherweight)

ACTION: Pump-action

FINISH: Matte blue receiver/barrel

CAPACITY: 4+1

Below: Model 37s have always had a classic game scene engraving on the receiver; this is the engraving from a current 28-gauge model. Courtesy Ithaca Gun Company.

Featherlight and Deerslayer Bottom Shucker
Produced: 1937–Present

In parts of upstate New York, I've hunted with a number of folks who only carried Ithaca Model 37s, whether they were hunting duck, grouse, or deer. The Ithaca Model 37 in the mid-twentieth century had a strong following, and for good reason. It worked well for either right- or left-handed shooters since empty shells are ejected from the bottom of the receiver. The pump-action was smooth and Featherlight models are easy to carry all day bird hunting, since the receiver is machined from aluminum. The Deerslayer models can do exactly that and are nearly as accurate as a rifle due to the fact the barrel to receiver fit is strong and true; plus the barrel is fully rifled. The Deerslayer III model boasts accuracy out to two hundred yards. Trap shooters also like this pump especially with a Monte Carlo style stock and 30-inch vent rib barrel. During World War II trench models were used. Even during the Vietnam War parkerized variants of the Model 37 were used. Law enforcement circles also used the Model 37 with special LE models built in the 1960s. New York City and Los Angeles police departments both used the Model 37. But the shotgun really shined in the hands of hunters since the Great Depression.

Originally the Model 37 was manufactured in Ithaca, New York, but over the years the company reorganized and locations changed. In 1987 the Model 37 name was changed to the Model 87, and just when the Model 37 was about to fade from memory the brand was revived in Sandusky, Ohio, and the name changed back to the Model 37.

The Model 37 is based on the Remington Model 17 designed by John Browning and John Pedersen. When the patents expired on the Remington Model 17 in 1937, Ithaca debuted the Model 37, and it has the distinction of being the longest production run for a pump-action shotgun. The design is unique in that shells are loaded or ejected from the bottom of the receiver. This makes the gun suitable for left- or right-handed shooters. Plus it means the mechanism is protected from the elements. Unlike many current pump-action and semiautomatic shotguns in which the trigger assembly and other guts of the mechanism are removed from the bottom of the receiver, on the Model 37 the trigger, bolt assemblies, and carrier are removed from the rear of the receiver necessitating removal of the stock. This design makes the Model 37 expensive to build, but those of us who have used the Model 37 know they are lithe and immensely pointable. Some two million and counting Model 37s have been built. I have a 16-gauge with a straight English style grip stock. I wouldn't trade it for the world.

Top: The current Model 37 Featherlight model has not changed much since it was introduced; why change if you don't have to?

Left: The 20-gauge Ultrafeatherlight tipped the scales at five pounds a generation ago, same as it does today.

Walther P38

First Military Double-Action Pistol
Produced: 1939–1945, 1957–2000 (P1 variant)

The P38 was the first pistol designed by Walther to fire the 9mm cartridge. Developed as replacement for the Luger P08, the P38 was designed for ease of production using stamped steel, alloy steels, and composite grips. The German militaries wanted a mass-produced pistol that was reliable, rugged, and suited for combat. The P38 was the answer. Though it was designed for ease in manufacturing, the design was cutting edge in 1938. Many modern pistol designs use features that were employed on the P38.

The P38 was the first combat pistol to use a combination of features starting with the pivoting, locking bolt short-recoil action. When the pistol is fired the barrel and slide move rearward in a linear fashion—the barrel does not tilt like in a 1911, SIG, Glock, or other Browning type action. Then the locking block stops the barrel movement but allows the slide to go rearward to eject a fired case, it cocks back the exposed hammer, and twin recoil springs bring the slide forward to chamber a round.

Other modern features found on the P38 include the double-/single-action trigger mechanism. The pistol can be safely carried with a round in the chamber and the hammer down allowing the operator to pull the trigger in double-action to fire the pistol. Subsequent shots are fired single-action. The safety lever located on the left side of the slide is swept downward to put the pistol on "S" or "safe" or pushed forward to expose an "F" for "fire." When the lever is placed on "safe" with the hammer cocked, the lever de-cocks the hammer. The loaded chamber indicator is a pin that protrudes from the top rear of the slide to give the operator tactile and visual indication that a round is in the chamber. The P38 also uses an open slide design forward of the breech face so ejection of empty cases is more reliable. The Beretta 92FS and current US Army issue M9 utilizes nearly all of these design characteristics. Since the grips meet to form the backstrap, less metal was required to build the pistol, making it lightweight. The sights on the P38 were large and well defined as one expects on a current combat pistol.

Specifications

CALIBER: 9mm

BARREL LENGTH: 4.9 inches

OA LENGTH: 8.5 inches

WEIGHT: 28 ounces (unloaded)

STOCK: Ribbed Bakelite

SIGHTS: Fixed, notch rear/blade front

ACTION: Short recoil, locked breech, semiautomatic

FINISH: Matte blue

CAPACITY: 8+1

Over one million P38s were produced by the end of the war in 1945. Walther, Mauser, and Spreewerk all manufactured the pistol during the war. Collectors note that markings with "ac" indicated a pistol produced by Walther. Mauser guns used either "byf" or "svw" codes. All Spreewerk guns are identified by "cyq."

After the war the P38 continued to serve in the German army and police, as well as other armies and law enforcement agencies around the world until 1992. The balance, accuracy, reliability, and safety features of the P38 and P1 were legendary.

Below: A pristine example of a WWII-era Walther P38 with issue holster. Courtesy Bishops Fine Guns.

Top: The P38 was a leap in technology and manufacturing compared to the P08 Luger it replaced. Courtesy Bishops Fine Guns.

Bottom: This post-war P38 is elaborately engraved with a German oak leaf pattern and sports checkered walnut grips. Courtesy Bishops Fine Guns.

Postwar P1

Postwar pistols differ from wartime specimens, since an aluminum frame replaced the steel frame models built during World War II, among other minor design changes. The new Walther was designated the P1 in 1957. In 1972 a design change included a steel hex bolt to reinforce the aluminum frame. The P1 was in service with the German *Bundeswehr* from 1957 through about 1992. Commercial variants were available in .22 LR, .30 Luger, and 9mm. The P1 came standard with black checkered grips. Large quantities of P38s that had been captured by the Soviets during the war were imported into the United States in 1990s; most of these pistols were inspected and refinished at the Izhevsk Mechanical Plant in Russia.

Beretta 92

The Beretta 92 was officially adopted by the US Military in 1985 as the M9. The 92 was designed in 1972 and produced continuously from 1975 in many model versions and calibers. Its origins are from early-twentieth-century Berettas where it received its characteristic open slide design. It borrowed the alloy frame and locking block barrel among other features from the WWII era Walther P38. Uncle Sam bought over 300,000 pistols in the first contract worth about $75 million dollars. By 2009 another 450,000 pistols were ordered by the government along with

Left: The sight system on the M9 is dot-and-post style. Barrel length is 4.9 inches. Magazine capacity is 15 rounds.

spare parts making the $220 million deal the largest US Military pistol contract awarded since WWII. The Marines variant is called the M9A1. After 30 years of US Military service starting in conflicts like the Invasion of Panama to the recent War in Afghanistan the M9 has proven its worth.

Right Top: The M9, like all 92 variants, has an external hammer that can be thumbed back for a single-action trigger pull. It also operates in double-action.

Bottom Right: The Marines' M9A1 was upgraded with a Picatinny MIL-STD-1913 accessory rail to attach tactical lights and laser aiming devices. The magazine well was aggressively beveled to assist fast reloads.

POST-WAR

Marlin Model 336

The Other Lever-Action Rifle
Produced: 1948–Present

If two lever-action rifles ever had a rivalry, it would be the Winchester 94 and the Marlin Model 336. The rivalry started back in late 1890s. The sad fact is the Model 336 has always played second fiddle to the Winchester 94, but what most deer and black bear hunters have known since 1948 is the Marlin is a simpler and more rugged lever-action beast basher. A rite of passage for young hunters in deer camp is the ability to silently cock the hammer on a lever-action rifle. More often than not it's with a Marlin.

The Marlin 336 descended from the Model 1893, then the Model 36. Marlin's lever-action rifles—the 36 and 336—competed head-to-head with the Winchester 94. The Marlin's side ejection easily allows mounting of optics, unlike the Winchester 94, which has top ejection. The 336 is also slightly heavier making the felt recoil from the .30-30 round—the most popular caliber—less noticeable. It is also more accurate than the Model 94 due to that heavier receiver. The lever design of the Model 336 is also simpler to disassemble than a Model 94. The success of this rifle is easily explained by the numbers produced; over six million 336 rifles have been built since it was introduced. It is the number two all-time selling American high-power sporting rifle. Yes, the Winchester Model 94 rifle is first.

In the 1950s Marlin introduced Micro-Groove rifling for jacketed bullets, which use many shallow grooves rather than the fewer deeper grooves of traditional rifling. The 336 uses a receiver made of forged steel and a round profile bolt that is chrome plated. It also incorporates use of coil springs in lieu of flat blade springs.

Numerous Marlin rifles have been built using the 336 receiver, including the XLR series with a 24-inch barrel and chambered in .308 Marlin Express, .338 Marlin Express, or .444 Marlin; the model 1896 in .45-70; and the popular

Specifications

CALIBER: .30-30 Winchester, .35 Remington (current models)

BARREL LENGTH: 18 or 20 inches (current models)

WEIGHT: 7 to 7.5 pounds (depending on barrel length/caliber)

STOCK: Checkered American black walnut (most common) or laminate hardwood

SIGHTS: Adjustable semi-buckhorn rear/hooded bead ramp front

ACTION: Lever-action, exposed hammer

FINISH: Blued or stainless

CAPACITY: 6-round tubular magazine

Above: Marlin's ads a few decades ago cut to the chase: the Model 336 "puts meat in the freezer."

Guide Guns with short barrels chambered in .45-70 and a big loop lever. The 336 rifles were also built under other names like Glenfield or Glenfield-Marlin for numerous big-box stores like Wal-Mart, Sears, Western Auto, and others. Today some of the big-box stores still do a brisk business in the Model 336 come deer season. You get your choice of either .30-30 or .35 Remington. At one time the 336 was chambered in .219 Zipper, .32 Special, .44 Magnum, and .410 shot bore. There is also a stainless model for you non-traditionalists.

My first deer rifle was a Model 336 with a half magazine tube chambered in .35 Remington. From Maine to upstate New York, the rifle never failed me, and that big .35 Remington bullet makes a big hole so tracking is easy. Enough said.

Above: This may be the perfect set-up in a deer rifle, a scoped 336 with sling, because it's easier to drag out when your rifle has a sling.

Guide Guns

The Model 1895SBL starts off with a 336 receiver in stainless steel and adds a stubby 18.5-inch barrel chambered in .45-70 Gov't and a big loop lever fitted on the underside. The XS Ghost Ring Sight offers fast aiming, or you can mount a scope on the Weaver-style rail. Use it for deer, pigs, black bear, moose, elk—whatever. Since 1998 Marlin has been making these short, fast handling lever actions. It has become cool again to hunt with a rifle your great-granddad used.

Above: The Guide Gun series like this Model 1895SBL is state of the art lever-action firepower.

AK-47

Most Widely Produced and Used Combat Rifle
Produced: 1949–1959

The AK-47 is found everywhere. It is the most common and the most reliable combat rifle ever designed. Over five hundred million have been manufactured, and though the newer variants have replaced it in some parts of the world, the AK-47 is still the king—or should I say tsar—of combat rifles. As much a symbol of rebellion as it is a symbol of repression, the AK-47 was born of war and Soviet engineering.

In the last year of World War II Mikhail Kalashnikov began designing a new battle rifle, and in 1946 he submitted it to the Soviet Army for field trials. In 1949 the rifle was adopted as the *Avtomat Kalashnikova* or as it is commonly known the AK, Kalash, or Kalashnikov. The rifle is renown for reliability under any condition—snow, sand, seawater, high humidity—as well as being inexpensive to produce. It is simple to operate and will run even if it is dirty. Likewise, it is simple to disassemble and reassemble. The effective range is out to 380 yards, and depending on what country manufactured the rifle, it has a service life up to fifteen thousand rounds.

Toward the end of World War II the Germans had developed a totally new style of weapon—the StG 44, or *Sturmgewehr 44,* which translated as "Assault Rifle 44." The StG 44 is considered the first modern assault rifle, and the AK-47 was greatly influenced by it. Both use an intermediate rifle round, a high-capacity magazine, and gas operating system, to name just a few similar features. What the StG 44 offered the operator was increased volume of firepower and greater range than a submachine gun, yet it was lighter and had less recoil than any combat rifle of the time. The Kalashnikov uses a long-stroke gas system. When a round is fired, gas from the burning powder is syphoned out of the barrel via a port to a piston above the barrel. The piston is driven back to operate the bolt carrier, eject the empty cartridge case, and cock the weapon; a recoil spring drives the bolt carrier forward, scraping a round out of the magazine and slamming it home into the chamber. Efficient and utterly reliable. The American-made M1 Garand used a similar system.

The stock on the AK-47 comes in either a fixed wood variant or a folding metal stock. The pistol grip offers good ergonomics for comfortable shooting

Specifications	
CALIBER: 7.62x39mm	
BARREL LENGTH: 16.3 inches	
OA LENGTH: 35 inches	
WEIGHT: 9.5 pounds (unloaded)	
STOCK: Smooth wood	
SIGHTS: Adjustable rear/winged front post	
ACTION: Gas-operated piston/ rotating bolt, select fire	
FINISH: Blued	
CAPACITY: 30-round detachable box magazine	
EFFECTIVE RANGE: 380 yards	

Above: The ubiquitous AK-47 is found wherever conflict or rebellion grows; these are AK-47 rifles seized in Iraq. Courtesy US Army.

Below: Russian troops carry a modern version of the AK-47, designated the AK-74.

and the characteristic curved magazine holds 30 rounds of 7.62x39mm ammunition. Original AK-47s used a machined receiver, though the design called for a stamped receiver. At the time of first production steel stamping machines needed to make the receivers were in low supply so machined receivers were used. In 1959 the AKM (*Avtomat Kalashnikova Modernizirovanniy*), or (literally translated) Automatic Kalashnikov Modernized, was produced using a stamped sheet steel receiver. The AKMs also feature a slanted muzzle brake and other slight design modifications.

In former Eastern Block countries like Poland, Albania, Ukraine, and Bulgaria, licensed versions of the AK were produced; versions also appeared in China, North Korea, Pakistan, and many African and South American countries. The quality of the rifle is greatly dependent on the country in which it was produced.

Commercially in the United States, semiautomatic AKs are imported and remanufactured to make them 922(r) compliant under United States Code. Though the AK is by no means a tack driver, it is a fairly accurate weapon capable of averaging 4–5 MOA at one hundred yards. The 7.62x39mm round has similar ballistics as the .30-30 Winchester round.

Above: The 5.45x39 caliber SLR-104FR, imported from Bulgaria and remanufactured by Arsenal Inc., is a classic example of a semiautomatic modern sporting rifle modeled after the AK-74 pattern.

922(r)-Compliant for Dummies

For a semiautomatic weapon to be compliant under 18 US Code § 922(r), the weapon—rifle or shotgun—must not have more than ten imported parts out of a list of twenty parts specified by the code. The twenty parts specified include:

1. Frames, receivers, receiver castings, forgings, or stampings
2. Barrels
3. Barrel extensions
4. Mounting blocks (trunnions)
5. Muzzle attachments
6. Bolts
7. Bolt carriers
8. Operating rods
9. Gas pistons
10. Trigger housings
11. Triggers
12. Hammers
13. Sears
14. Disconnectors
15. Butt stocks
16. Pistol grips
17. Forearms, hand guards
18. Magazine bodies
19. Followers
20. Floorplates

Right: This Russian marine wields an AK-74.

AK-74 Variant

The AKM was replaced by the AK-74 in 1974, hence the nomenclature. The AK-74 is an adaptation of the AKM that uses a smaller 5.45x39mm cartridge, which provides better range and accuracy. The AKM and AK-74 share about 50 percent of the same parts. This rifle was first used by the Soviets in the Soviet War in Afghanistan and has been used by the Russians ever since.

Ruger Mark I

Everyman's .22 Pistol
Produced: 1949–Present

A .22 rimfire pistol was part of every sportsman's kit in the mid-twentieth century. The Colt Woodsman competed with High Standard models like the Olympic, Supermatic, Field-King, and others. As much as the shooting public liked .22 LR semiautomatic pistols, these pistols were becoming increasingly expensive to produce. Bill Ruger, part inventor, part self-taught engineer, and firearm enthusiast, had an idea to make an inexpensive .22 pistol that still had the quality of the Colt and High Standard pistols. His idea became the Standard pistol, and it went on to become one of the bestselling and most popular .22 pistols ever manufactured.

The Standard pistol and Mark I pistol trace their lineage back to Bill Ruger's garage in 1949, when he duplicated a Japanese Baby Nambu pistol that a US Marine acquired as a souvenir during World War II. Ruger tweaked the bolt system from the Nambu, got together some venture capital from Alex Sturm, and started building and selling a .22 rimfire pistol in 1949 that cost $37.50. You could order one by mail at the time. Shooters liked the nostalgic style that was similar to the iconic Luger P08.

The Standard was the first Ruger rimfire pistol to be introduced, and it used a novel manufacturing process. The frame was made of two stamped steel sheet pieces welded together with a cylindrical

Below: Many sportsmen found an ad like this in the back of hunting and fishing magazines starting in 1949.

the .22 **RUGER** pistol

The .22 Ruger Pistol represents the first overall improvement in automatic pistol design since the Browning patent of 1905.

For simplicity, strength and handsomeness it has no equal.

A cylindrical bolt moving in a tubular receiver provides a strong, simple action with unmoving sights. It can be dismantled in five seconds.

The Ruger Pistol weighs 2¼ pounds and measures 9 inches with a 4¾ inch barrel. It fills a man's hand fully and comfortably. The grips are sharply checkered hard rubber; the trigger is broad and grooved. It has a positive safety catch and detachable magazine holding nine .22 caliber long rifle cartridges.

The reader is invited to send for a free leaflet describing the Ruger Pistol in detail.

STURM, RUGER & CO., INC.
SOUTHPORT, CONNECTICUT

bolt located inside the frame. The cylindrical bolt system ensures better alignment than conventional slide pistols thereby giving the pistol better accuracy. The pistol uses a simple blow-back mechanism. Fire a round and the force pushes back the bolt to eject the empty case and cock the hammer, and the recoil spring drives the bolt forward grabbing a round out of the magazine and slamming it into the chamber.

Right: The Ruger Standard and Mark I stressed its quality and low price.

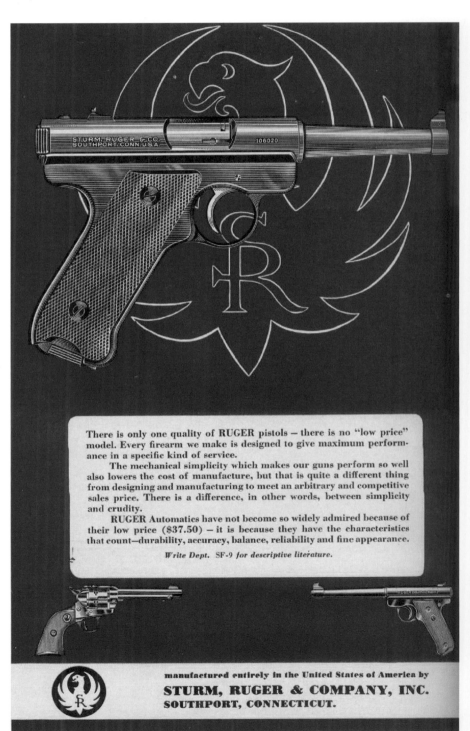

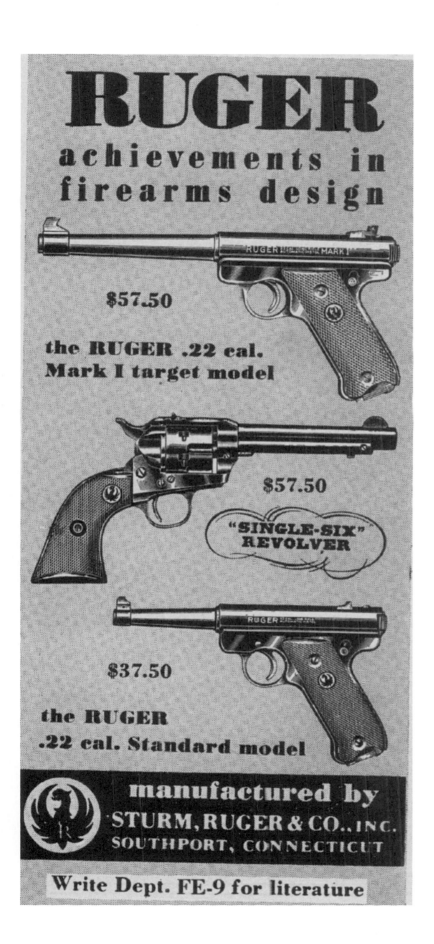

RUGER
achievements in firearms design

$57.50

the RUGER .22 cal.
Mark I target model

$57.50

"SINGLE-SIX"
REVOLVER

$37.50

the RUGER
.22 cal. Standard model

manufactured by
STURM, RUGER & CO., INC.
SOUTHPORT, CONNECTICUT

Write Dept. FE-9 for literature

Left: Ruger had the .22 rimfire handgun market covered with semiautomatic and revolver models at a very reasonable price.

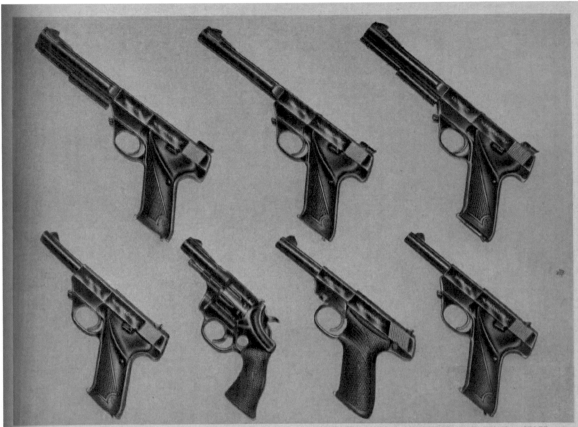

The Standard instantly became a plinker's favorite gun. The Mark I Target began selling in 1951 for $57.50. It had a longer 6.875-inch barrel and an adjustable rear sight with a front blade sight under cut for less glare. Now target shooters had an inexpensive entry pistol for small-bore pistol competition. Since that time the Standard pistol evolved to the MK II in 1982 and later the MK III, which features a loaded chamber indicator, magazine release behind the trigger guard, magazine disconnect safety, and other details. The MK III 22/45 models use a polymer grip frame with the same grip angle as a 1911 pistol.

If there is any complaint about these pistols, it arises from the disassembly procedure—sort of a puzzle. Be patient the first few times. As they say practice makes perfect.

Above: The Mark III is the most current model, featuring a thumb-actuated magazine release, magazine disconnector, and loaded chamber indicator.

Opposite page: High Standard was one of the preeminent .22 rimfire handgun manufacturers in the mid-twentieth century with a variety of models, as this 1956 ad displays.

Colt Woodsman

If the Ruger Standard and Mark I were the everyman's .22 pistol, then the Colt Woodsman was the .22 pistol most aspired to own. Manufactured from 1915 through 1977, the Woodsman evolved over the decades until there was nary a camper or hiker who didn't own or want to own a Woodsman. The Standard model had a 6.5-in. barrel, and the Sport model had a 4.5-inch barrel. Ernest Hemingway had Woodsman, and used it to kill marlin before bringing the fish onboard.

Specifications	
CALIBER: .22 LR	
BARREL LENGTH: 4.75 inches	
OA LENGTH: 9 inches	
WEIGHT: 35 ounces (unloaded)	
STOCK: Checkered polymer	
SIGHTS: Fixed, notch rear/blade front	
ACTION: Blow back, semiautomatic	
FINISH: Blue	
CAPACITY: 9+1	

Left: A first issue Colt Woodsman Standard model was a simple design that was built on a forged frame. Courtesy Bishops Fine Guns.

Remington Model 870

Greatest Pump Shotgun Ever Produced: 1950–Present

The Remington Model 870 pump-action shotgun has sold over ten million and counting. It is versatile—the assortment of barrels ranges from long goose gun tubes to short home defenders—and it is reliable. It helps that the 870's good looks and ease of handling—they call it Wingmaster for a reason—help make it America's greatest pump shotgun.

Bird and duck hunters alike appreciate the 870. Swap out the bird barrel for one that is rifled and has iron sights, and a cantilever rail for a scope, and you have a good deer gun. Many law enforcement and military agencies worldwide use the Remington 870. Millions have been produced and sold for good reason.

Like many Remington firearms, the idea behind the Model 870 was to produce a more cost effective alternative to the Remington Model 31. Though the Model 31 was popular with hunters and clay shooters, the firearm required extensive machining. It was costly to produce and it competed against the Winchester Model 12, another extremely popular pump at the time. When the 870 was introduced, it offered a more modern, streamlined look. The 870 was also built to take abuse and be reliable. Accidentally drop an 870 in a swamp outside your duck blind or forget it in the pickup truck bed as you bump along a dirt road at 50 mph, and it will still work every time. Law enforcement agencies like the FBI, California Highway Patrol, Pennsylvania State Police, US Border Patrol, US Secret Service, and branches of the US Military all use one form or another of the Model 870.

The 870 pump-action incorporates dual-action bars for a non-binding smooth pump. Shells are loaded from the bottom of the receiver into a tubular magazine under

Below: A member of the Maritime Safety and Security team wields a tactical 870.

Above: The versatility of the Model 870 (from top to bottom) Express Deer gun; Super Magnum for geese; Wingmaster for upland birds; Express Tactical for LE, military, or home defense; and Super Magnum with red dot sight for turkey hunting.

Specifications

GAUGE: 12, 16, 20, 28, .410

BARREL LENGTH: 18 to 30 inches

OA LENGTH: 48.5 inches (28-in. barrel, 12-gauge)

WEIGHT: 7.5 lbs. (28-in. barrel, 12-gauge)

STOCK: Glossy walnut or synthetic

SIGHTS: HiViz or metal bead front, metal bead mid rib

ACTION: Pump-action

FINISH: Blued, nickel, Mossy Oak camo or matte blue receiver/blued, camo or matte blue barrel

CAPACITY: 4+1 (3+1 for Express variants using 3-1/2-in. shells)

the barrel. The receivers are sized for 12-gauge and 20-gauge; 16-gauge models used the 12-gauge size receiver, and small gauges like .410 and 28 use the 20-gauge receiver. The 870 is also one of those shotguns that transitioned from fixed choke barrels to barrels that use multi-choke tubes. In 1986 Remington introduced the Rem Choke system of screw-in choke tubes.

There are numerous variants of the Model 870 for hunters, from the plain-Jane Express variant with matte blue and hardwood or synthetic stock to the Wingmaster with a deep blue metal finish and walnut stock. On the tactical end of the spectrum is the Model 870 Express Tactical, outfitted with either Magpul or Blackhawk stocks and forends to the SPS Marine Magnum with an electrolysis nickel plating on the metal and synthetic stock.

The ability to easily replace the barrel for different uses means the 870 was extremely versatile compared to the other pump guns of the day. It was also inexpensive. For over sixty-five years the 870 has set the benchmark for inexpensive reliable pump guns.

Below: A magazine ad from last century depicting the Wingmaster as the best pump shotgun for the price.

Ruger Single-Six

Building a Better Single-Action Revolver
Produced: 1953–Present

There probably isn't a plinker in America who hasn't fired a Ruger Single-Six or one of its many variants. Tens of thousands of these small SA revolvers have been produced since 1953. Back in the 1950s people huddled around the TV with anticipation to watch *Wagon Train, Hopalong Cassidy, The Lone Ranger, Rawhide,* and numerous others. Cowboy TV shows were big back then, and Bill Ruger had a big idea: Why not produce a cowboy-style gun? The Single-Six was a revolver to meet that demand, and it (and its many variants) have proven to be a tremendous success. From plinkers to small game hunters, the Single-Six is a fun and safe single-action revolver that is built to last many trips to the local sand pit to plink tin cans or travel on a hunter's hip in search of bushy-tail squirrels. What makes these such popular revolvers are calibers—mostly inexpensive rimfire calibers like .17 HMR, .22 LR, and .22 WMR. Low recoil, good accuracy, and inexpensive cartridges means these revolvers are shot a lot and are great guns to introduce to new shooters.

The original Single-Six used a mechanism similar to that of the Colt SAA. It was a six-shot single-action revolver with no safety. These are referred to as "old models" or "three screw models," since they used three screws in the frame. One of the Colt SAA's weaknesses is the use of flat

Below: This ad from 1958 stressed the quality and workmanship of the Single-Six and the new patent Ruger mechanism.

THE NEW RUGER .22

"SINGLE-SIX" REVOLVER

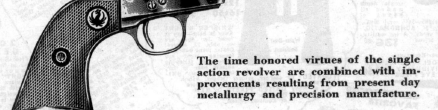

The time honored virtues of the single action revolver are combined with improvements resulting from present day metallurgy and precision manufacture.

No other type of revolver possesses the wonderful grip, balance, and mechanical simplicity of the single action. In the new RUGER "SINGLE-SIX" all these legendary qualities are retained and in addition many positive improvements in construction have been achieved.

Although the gun is probably the strongest revolver ever made it is produced exclusively in .22 caliber. With this effective and economical cartridge the RUGER "SINGLE-SIX," derived from an historical American pattern, offers unique satisfaction to the sportsman and shooting enthusiast of today.

 Uses .22 short, long or long rifle ammunition.

Specifications

Barrel: Length, 5½", diameter of breech, 11/16", diameter of muzzle, ⅝", 6 groove rifling, 14" twist, assembled to frame by 20 pitch screw threads.

Action: Six shots, recessed chambers, cylinder dia. 1-13/32", cylinder length 1⅜". Solid frame of chrome molybdenum steel, rod ejector.

Springs: Best quality music wire springs throughout, no leaf springs.

Weight: 35 ozs.

Overall Length: 10⅞".

Sights: Fixed, wide blade (.093") patridge style front, precision machined, square notch rear. Rear sight mounted in dovetail in flat top frame. Sight radius, 6⅛".

Ignition Mechanism: Alloy steel firing pin mounted in frame.

Grips: Moulded hard rubber having exceptional resistance to impact; black gloss finish, sharp diamond checkering.

Finish: Polished all over and blued.

Price: $57.50 (Retail List).

This gun is now in production and will be available through all established dealers, but all orders cannot be filled simultaneously and a delayed delivery may be unavoidable. Descriptive literature will be sent upon request. Write Dept. AR-6.

manufactured by
STURM, RUGER & COMPANY, INC.
SOUTHPORT, CONNECTICUT, U. S. A.

Left: In stainless steel this single-action revolver offers great looks and reliability.

Opposite Page: From 1953 the Single-Six advertisements stressed the classic style and the modern improvements of this single-action revolver.

springs. Bill Ruger used music wire coil springs in his Single-Six to make the revolvers more reliable. The first models had a flat loading gate but that was changed to the Colt SAA-style loading gate around 1957. Originals had a 5.5-inch barrel and used an alloy grip frame. Collectors call these XR3 grip frames. Chambered in .22 LR—it also could use .22 Short and .22 Long cartridges—the Single-Six had black checkered rubber grips with a black Ruger logo medallion. The rear sight was drift adjustable and the finish was blue.

In 1973 the mechanism of the Single-Six was modified to incorporate a transfer bar. Another weakness in the Colt SAA is the lack of any safety. The Old Model/Three Screw Single-Six was best carried loaded with five cartridges and the hammer resting on an empty chamber like a Colt SAA. The new mechanism placed a transfer bar between the hammer and the firing pin at the exact moment the trigger is fully pulled to the rear. Thus the hammer hits the transfer bar, which in turn transfers the blow to the firing pin to discharge the gun. These revolvers are referred to as New Model Single-Six.

Current model variants include a centerfire option chambered in .327 Federal Magnum. Over the years the Single-Six has also been chambered in .32 H&R Magnum, but to most it is a rimfire. A Single-Nine variant is chambered in .22 WMR, and a Single-Ten squeezes ten .22 LR chambers in the revolver. The Convertible models offer two cylinders, one chambered in .22 LR and the other in .22 WMR. Swapping cylinders takes seconds and offers more power in the .22 WMR. A Hunter model with a 7.5-inch barrel is set up to easily mount a scope or a red dot sight.

Specifications

CALIBER: .17 HMR, .22 LR, .22 WMR, .32 H&R Magnum, and .327 Federal Magnum

BARREL LENGTH: 4.63, 5.5, 6.5, 7.5, and 9.5 inches

OA LENGTH: 11 inches (5.5-inch barrel)

WEIGHT: 33 ounces (5.5-inch barrel/blued), 39 ounces (5.5-inch barrel/stainless)

STOCK: Smooth hardwood or checkered hard rubber

SIGHTS: Adjustable rear/fixed ramp front

ACTION: Single-action

FINISH: Blued or stainless steel

CAPACITY: 6, 7 (.327 Federal Magnum), 9 (Single-Nine), 10 (Single-Ten)

Ruger Bearcat

Small, lightweight, and chambered in .22 LR, the Ruger Bearcat has been used by hunters, hikers, and campers since 1958. A cougar and a bear are roll-engraved on the unfluted cylinder. Like the Single-Six, the Bearcat has undergone design changes over the years. The Bearcat 3rd

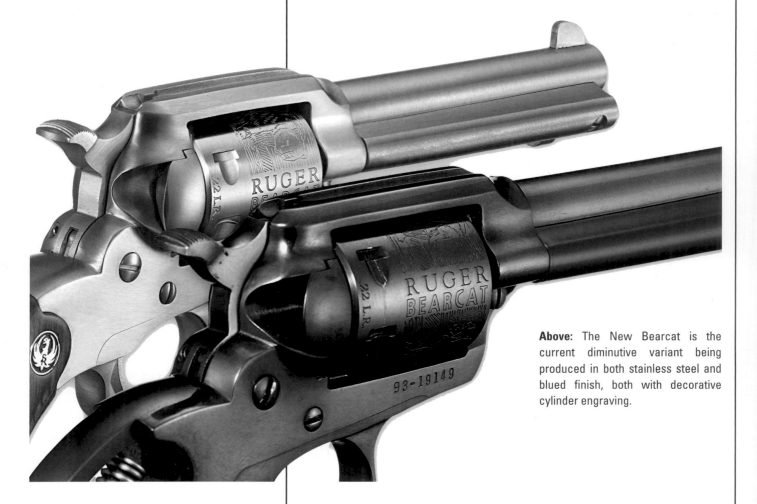

Above: The New Bearcat is the current diminutive variant being produced in both stainless steel and blued finish, both with decorative cylinder engraving.

Issue incorporates the safety transfer bar. The Bearcat design is based on the classic Remington Model 1875 and Model 1890 revolvers. Bill Ruger liked old guns, and it is evident in many of his designs.

Colt Python

Cadillac of American Revolvers
Produced: 1955–2005

The Colt Python is one of the finest production revolvers ever built. Hand-fitted with the action honed, the Python was known for its accuracy, smooth trigger pull, and tight lock-up. When it debuted in 1955 it was an immediate success. Not only was the action exceptionally smooth, the revolver incorporated features—like a full-length lug under the barrel, excellent adjustable sights, and the frame size—that are today standard in many revolvers. The Smith & Wesson L-frame is very close to the Python's I-frame. Like all Colts, the cylinder rotates into the frame to make the cylinder-to-frame lockup stronger. By contrast the cylinders of Smith & Wesson revolvers rotate counterclockwise. The finish choices included a polished Royal Blue that set the benchmark in steel blue finish. Nickel and stainless steel were also offered.

Chambered in .357 Magnum the revolver had enough heft so felt recoil was tolerable. While the short-barrel variants were in the holsters of lawmen, the longer-barreled models were used by target shooters and hunters. Collectors and shooters covet these revolvers. If you find one, even if it is a beater, it will most likely be better than anything new you can buy today. No wonder they have been called the Rolls Royce or Cadillac of revolvers.

Specifications

CALIBER: .357 Magnum

BARREL LENGTH: 2.5, 3, 4 (most common), 6, and 8 inches

OA LENGTH: 9.5 inches (4-inch barrel)

WEIGHT: 43.2 ounces (4-inch barrel, unloaded)

STOCK: Checkered walnut or textured rubber

SIGHTS: Adjustable rear/ramp front

ACTION: Single/double-action

FINISH: Blue (most common), nickel, or stainless

CAPACITY: 6

Right: No lie, the Python was compared to the Cadillac in this 1956 ad.

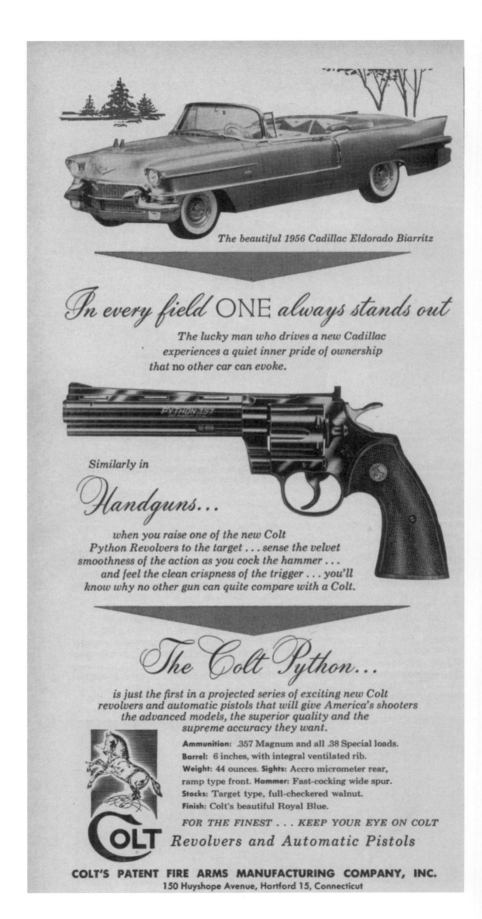

The beautiful 1956 Cadillac Eldorado Biarritz

In every field ONE *always stands out*

The lucky man who drives a new Cadillac experiences a quiet inner pride of ownership that no other car can evoke.

Similarly in

Handguns...

when you raise one of the new Colt Python Revolvers to the target . . . sense the velvet smoothness of the action as you cock the hammer . . . and feel the clean crispness of the trigger . . . you'll know why no other gun can quite compare with a Colt.

The Colt Python...

is just the first in a projected series of exciting new Colt revolvers and automatic pistols that will give America's shooters the advanced models, the superior quality and the supreme accuracy they want.

Ammunition: .357 Magnum and all .38 Special loads. **Barrel:** 6 inches, with integral ventilated rib. **Weight:** 44 ounces. **Sights:** Accro micrometer rear, ramp type front. **Hammer:** Fast-cocking wide spur. **Stocks:** Target type, full-checkered walnut. **Finish:** Colt's beautiful Royal Blue.

FOR THE FINEST . . . KEEP YOUR EYE ON COLT

COLT *Revolvers and Automatic Pistols*

COLT'S PATENT FIRE ARMS MANUFACTURING COMPANY, INC.
150 Huyshope Avenue, Hartford 15, Connecticut

Top: The stainless steel models were produced from 1983 through 2006; this one sports a 6-inch barrel.

Middle: The 8-inch barrel models like this one with a nickel finish were used for target shooting and hunting. Courtesy Bishops Fine Guns.

Bottom: This 4-inch barrel model shows the fine Colt Royal Blue finish. Courtesy Stephen Z.

Above: The Python wasn't the first Colt revolver to use a snake name; other models were called Anaconda, Viper, Cobra, and Diamondback.

Smith & Wesson Model 29

"The Most Powerful Handgun in the World"
Produced: 1955–Present

What Ian Fleming's James Bond character did for the Walther PPK, Clint Eastwood's *Dirty Harry* series of movies did for the Smith & Wesson Model 29. It elevated a revolver most shooters had already known about and admired into a pop culture icon. I'm sure Elmer Keith, the original person to push for the Model 29 and .44 Magnum, gave two hoots about *Dirty Harry*.

The revolver that made everyone's day was built on Smith & Wesson's N-frame. The N-frame was used to produce the first .357 Magnum revolver in 1935, known as the Registered Magnum. S&W chose to chamber the powerful .357 Magnum cartridge in a six-shot revolver built from this large, heavy-duty carbon-steel N-frame. Almost immediately the Registered Magnum was adopted by the Kansas City Police Department, and other LE agencies soon followed. To say the revolver and caliber combination was successful is an understatement. When introduced at the height of the Great

Above: The Model 29 revolver chambered in .44 Magnum and with a 6-inch barrel is iconic.

Specifications

CALIBER: .44 Magnum

BARREL LENGTH: 3, 4, 5, 5.5, 6.5, 7.5, 8.75, and 10.62 inches

OA LENGTH: 11 inches (5.5-inch barrel)

WEIGHT: 33 ounces (5.5-inch barrel/blued), 39 ounces (5.5-inch barrel/stainless)

STOCK: Smooth hardwood or checkered hard rubber

SIGHTS: Adjustable rear/fixed ramp front

ACTION: Single-action

FINISH: Blued or stainless steel

CAPACITY: 6, 7 (.327 Federal Magnum), 9 (Single-Nine), and 10 (Single-Ten)

Below: Buffalo Bore loads .44 Magnum cartridges using Elmer Keith's bullet design, a 255-grain semi-wadcutter.

Depression, the revolver cost sixty dollars and Smith & Wesson had a hard time filling these special order items. The big N-frame had a pinned barrel, counter-bored cylinder chambers, and checkering across the top strap of the frame and barrel.

Over the years the revolver went through several name changes. In the late 1930s the model name was changed to ".357 Magnum." Eventually it would become known as the Model 27 when S&W started to use numeric model names in the mid-1950s.

General George S. Patton carried a .357 Magnum model and outfitted it with ivory grips and a Tyler T-grip to fill that gap between the rear of the trigger guard and front strap. He called it his "killing gun." From the 1940s through the 1960s, many FBI agents used a 3.5-inch barrel model. J. Edgar Hoover is said to have owned one of the first Registered Magnums. Noted gun writer Skeeter Skelton was known to favor a 5-inch model.

Keith, a gun writer and handloader, had been loading hot cartridges for the .44 Special and running them through his S&W Triple Locks, the nickname for S&W's .44 Hand Ejector 1st Model New Century revolvers. The nickname comes from a third locking lug on the crane. They were well built and made to shoot big bore .44 Special cartridges. Keith juiced up his handloaded cartridges and found the added power and performance made a great hunting round or good protection in bear country when dangerous game was present. The .44 Magnum is similar to the .44 Special, except the .44 Magnum uses a longer case for more powder. The Model 29 was the revolver Keith cajoled out of S&W executives, and it proved to completely change the nature of the

Top: Keith ran his handloads through a S&W Triple Lock. Courtesy Hatchetfish.

handgun and revolver. The Model 29 and .44 Magnum allowed hunters to hunt big game with a handgun in a caliber that offered accuracy and excellent down-range power Like Dirty Harry said in 1971: ". . . this is the most powerful handgun in the world . . . ."

S&W's Five-Shot Hand Cannon

The S&W Model 500 debuted in 2003, replacing the Model 29 as top gun status. The Model 500 is chambered in .50 S&W. Winchester loads 400-grain bullets with a muzzle velocity of 1675 fps and muzzle energy

of 2877 ft-lbs. To contain this nuclear reaction, S&W came out with the supersized and super-strong X-frame. The revolver is huge. There's a reason some models come with a sling.

Ruger Blackhawk

A Built-Better Six-Shooter
Produced: 1955–Present

The Blackhawk rode into town when *Gunsmoke*, *The Lone Ranger*, *Bonanza*, and other TV westerns were on prime time. The exact date was 1955. With Ruger's success with the Single-Six .22 LR rimfire single-action revolver, the

Right: The Blackhawk and Single-Six were, and still are, the most robust single-action revolvers available.

company decided to sell centerfire single-action pistols. They sold bucketfuls of them. Though based on the Colt SAA, the Blackhawk made the revolver much stronger and affordable.

Ruger uses an investment cast method to manufacturer the alloy steel cylinder frames, aluminum grip frames, coiled springs throughout, and hammer-forged barrels. The first Blackhawks off the assembly line are referred to as Flattop models because the frame strap along the top of the cylinder was flat. The design was tweaked and the top strap was beefed up to help protect the rear sight. These single-actions evolved into what is called the "three screw" models, which used three screws in the side of the frame. They are loaded like the Colt SAA: with

Specifications

CALIBER: .30 Carbine, .327 Fed. Mag., .357 Magnum, .357 Rem. Mag., .41 Rem. Magnum, .44 Special, .44 Magnum, .45 Colt

BARREL LENGTH: 4.62, 5.5, 6.6, 7.5, or 10.5 inches

OA LENGTH: 13.38 inches (7.5-inch barrel)

WEIGHT: 40 ounces (7.5-inch barrel)

STOCK: Smooth wood or checkered rubber

SIGHTS: Adjustable rear/ramp blade front

ACTION: Single-action

FINISH: Blued or stainless

CAPACITY: 6

Left: In the 1950s everyone was getting their cowboy on; primetime TV ran a slew of Westerns.

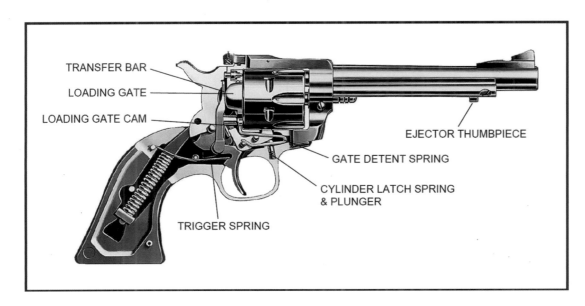

TRANSFER BAR

LOADING GATE

LOADING GATE CAM

EJECTOR THUMBPIECE

GATE DETENT SPRING

CYLINDER LATCH SPRING & PLUNGER

TRIGGER SPRING

Top: The internal mechanism of the Blackhawk is different, using modern coil springs and high strength alloys, than the Colt SAA.

Right: The flat bar over the firing pin is the transfer bar; it moves up into position when the hammer is fully cocked and the trigger is pulled.

hammer on half cock the loading gate is opened, then the cylinder rotated to fill the first chamber, skip the next chamber, and then fill the remaining chambers. It is safely carried with hammer down on an empty chamber. In 1973 the New Model Blackhawk debuted utilizing a transfer bar that prevents the pistol from firing a round if the revolver is dropped on its hammer. To load the New Model Blackhawks only the loading gate needs to be opened to rotate and load the chambers. These model are also safe to carry with all chambers loaded. These models can be identified by the two screws in the side of the frame.

The Blackhawk is a robust revolver with excellent sights that is perfect for cowboy action shooting, hunting, plinking and protecting the ranch.

The Other Blackhawks

Mechanically similar to the Blackhawk, the Blackhawk Bisley features a different grip shape. The Super Blackhawk is chambered in .44 Magnum and is recognizable due to its unfitted cylinder and squared off trigger guard. The Vaquero is similar to the New Model Blackhawk but the mechanisms are different and they do not share many parts.

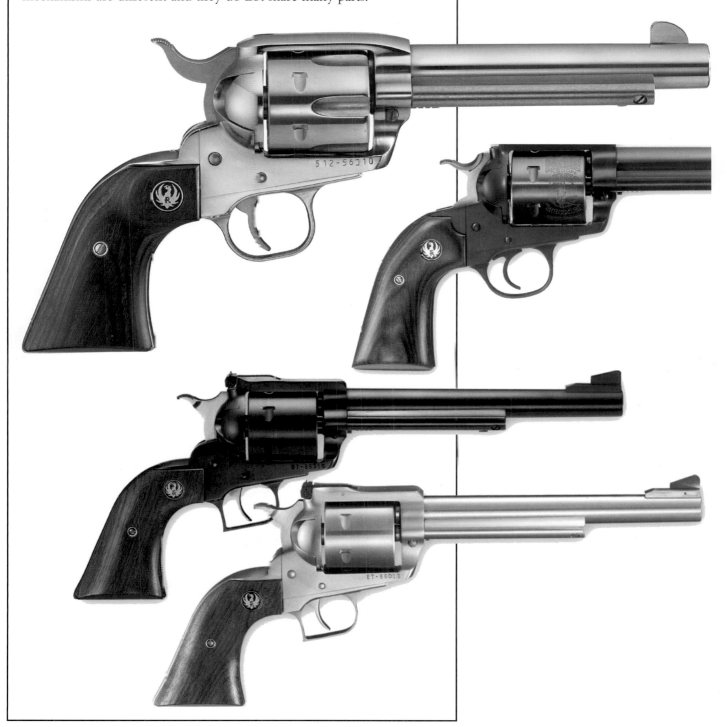

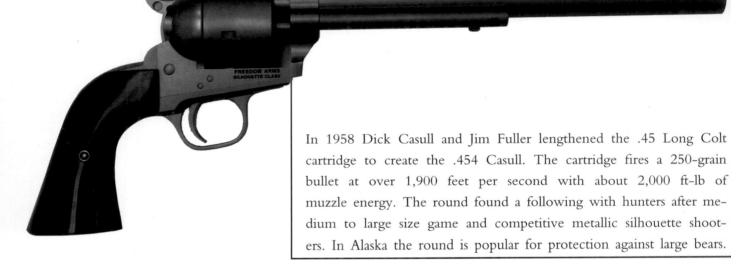

Freedom Arms Model 83

The Ruger Super Blackhawk in .44 Magnum is a powerful pistol with powerful range and powerful recoil. More is better, as they say, and the Freedom Arms Model 83 is a five-shot single-action revolver chambered in .454 Casull—a wrist cracking, bone busting caliber that took handgun hunting to next level.

In 1958 Dick Casull and Jim Fuller lengthened the .45 Long Colt cartridge to create the .454 Casull. The cartridge fires a 250-grain bullet at over 1,900 feet per second with about 2,000 ft-lb of muzzle energy. The round found a following with hunters after medium to large size game and competitive metallic silhouette shooters. In Alaska the round is popular for protection against large bears.

Above: This Freedom Arms revolver is set up for long range metallic silhouette shooting competitions.

Weatherby Mark V

Speed Kills
Produced: 1957–Present

Weatherby Mark V rifles can be defined as iconic, luxurious, and high performance. It was the late 1940s when Roy Weatherby began building rifles in his California shop. These rifles used what were then Weatherby's wildcat cartridges based on his design philosophy that lightweight bullets traveling at high speed provided the best terminal performance. Those cartridges, with their unique double radius venturi shoulder design, became a line of proprietary cartridges with calibers ranging from the diminutive .224 up through the colossal .460. The .257 Weatherby Magnum is said to have

Top: The Weatherby Mark V Deluxe has a style all its own and a slew of proprietary calibers.

Right: Roy Weatherby was the consummate wildcatter; here he examines a tree he shot with one of the rifles chambered in his proprietary calibers.

Specifications

CALIBER: (Proprietary)
.224 Weatherby Magnum,
.240 Weatherby Magnum,
.257 Weatherby Magnum,
270 Weatherby Magnum,
7mm Weatherby Magnum,
.300 Weatherby Magnum,
.30-378 Weatherby Magnum,
.340 Weatherby Magnum,
.338-378 Weatherby Magnum,
375 Weatherby Magnum,
.378 Weatherby Magnum,
.416 Weatherby Magnum, .
460 Weatherby Magnum;
(standard) .22-250 Remington,
.243 Winchester, .25-06 Remington,
.270 Winchester,
7mm-08 Remington,
7mm Remington Magnum, .
308 Winchester, .30-06 Springfield,
.300 Winchester Magnum,
.338-06, .338 Winchester Magnum,
.375 H&H Magnum,
.416 Remington Magnum,
.458 Winchester Magnum, .458 Lott

BARREL LENGTH: 22, 24, 26, and 28 inches (depending on caliber)

OA LENGTH: 46.63 inches (26-inch barrel)

WEIGHT: 7.25 pounds (26-inch barrel)

STOCK: Composite or AAA fancy walnut

SIGHTS: None, drilled and tapped

been Roy's personal favorite. In 1957 the hot rod cartridges were mated to Weatherby's proprietary action, the Mark V, built to be stronger, safer, and able to withstand the tremendous pressure of Weatherby's high-velocity cartridges. The action features nine locking lugs and a 54-degree bolt lift. If the cartridges and action were not unique enough, Weatherby's stock has a distinct Monte Carlo comb sculpted from either fancy wood or hand-laminated with composites or synthetics. Initial production of the Mark V started in California, but European and Asian manufacturers have also built the Mark V. It is currently produced in the USA.

Above: The Weatherby Mark V bolt has nine locking lugs (far left), next is a Mauser style control feed bolt, then a three-lug bolt from a T/C Icon, and a bolt from a Remington Model 700.

Range Certified

Weatherby is so focused on accuracy they offer a line of Range Certified rifles that guarantee sub-MOA accuracy of 0.99-inches or less from a three-shot group at one hundred yards.

ACTION: Bolt-action, 9-lug (magnum calibers), 6-lug (standard calibers)

FINISH: Blued, matte blue, stainless steel, or flat dark earth Create

CAPACITY: 2+1, 3+1 (magnum calibers), 5+1 (standard calibers)

Left: The Mark V Arroyo RC features a factory-tuned, fully-adjustable trigger and is signed and certified to shoot sub-MOA groups by Ed or Adam Weatherby.

Savage Model 110

Unassuming Tack Driver
Produced: 1958–Present

Let's face the truth: at one time, Savage bolt-actions were ugly. The wood stocks looked like a high school freshman's first woodworking project, the triggers were gosh-awful, and the barrel nut that held the barrel to the receiver was butt-ugly. The accuracy of the Model 110 rifles made this aesthetically displeasing rifle absolutely beautiful.

The Model 110 was developed in the mid–1950s and offered commercially in 1958, making it the oldest continuously manufactured bolt-action rifle in the United States. The bottom line with these rifles is they are accurate, reliable, and inexpensive. The Model 110 was designed from the beginning for ease in manufacturing and assembly. Savage in the past few decades has turned their ugly stepchild of a rifle into a series of rifles that are not only beautiful but push the envelope on accuracy in an inexpensive rifle.

In 1966 it was reengineered to yet again make it more cost effective to produce. By 1998 another design change came, and this is when Savage came into its own.

Certain characteristics of the Model 110 series make it sing. First, there are the button-rifled barrels. For a barrel to be accurate, it needs to be a perfectly consistent tube. The barrel is fully threaded into the action and locked in place via a barrel locknut. This helps shooters better adjust headspace tolerances and also contributes to better accuracy. The floating bolt head is unique. The Savage bolt head is made of two parts that allow for a slight amount of play or

Below: The 110 Trophy Hunter XP package includes a Model 110 rifle with a factory-installed Nikon 3-9x40mm scope with BDC reticle.

float to provide the best lug engagement in the recess of the receiver and lock the cartridge in the chamber. When you purchase a custom rifle from Savage, the builder spends time ensuring the bolt is tuned and squared up to the receiver. Savage controls the rifle's headspace exactly with zero tolerance by placing a minimum headspace gauge in the barrel's chamber. The bolt is then closed and locked into the receiver. The barrel is threaded into the receiver until it stops, and the barrel nut locks down the barrel and receiver. Savage's AccuStock uses an aluminum rail system to secure the action to the stock in three directions. Keeping the action in place ensures excellent accuracy. AccuTrigger, introduced in 2003, was designed with an integrated release, a thin blade in the center of the trigger that must be completely depressed to fire the rifle. Though this feature reduces legal liability for Savage, it gives the shooter a trigger that can be adjusted from six ounces to six pounds.

The Savage Model 10, a short action rifle, is based on the Model 110, a long action rifle. The Model 10/110 LE Series and Model 12/112 Target/Varmint Series rifles, though similar in appearance, have slightly different bolts and receivers. Numerous models from the Model 10/110, 11/111, 14/114, and 16/116 series employ the same bolt style, though finish, stock, and magazine types differ.

Some of my smallest groups have been fired with Savage rifles straight off the assembly line.

Specifications

CALIBER: .222 Remington, .223 Remington, .22-250 Remington, .243 Winchester, .250-3000 Savage, .25-06 Remington, 6.5 Creedmoor, 6.5x284 Norma, .270 Winchester, 7mm-08, 7x57mm, 7mm Remington Magnum, .300 Savage, .30-06 Springfield, .308 Winchester, .300 Winchester Magnum, .338 Winchester Magnum, .338 Lapua Magnum

BARREL LENGTH: 20, 22, 24, and 26 inches (depending on caliber)

WEIGHT: 6.25 to 15.75 lb. (depending on caliber/barrel length)

STOCK: Checkered wood or polymer (standard)

SIGHTS: Optic ready

ACTION: Bolt, push feed, two-lug

FINISH: Blued or stainless

CAPACITY: 3+1 or 4+1 (depending on caliber)

Left: The author fired this group at one hundred yards from a Model 11/111 Long Range Hunter chambered in 6.5 Creedmoor.

Top: Savage Model 110 rifles are accurate due to exactly managing the headspace in each rifle, as well as other features.

Going Long

The Savage Model 12 Palma is purpose-built for long-range target shooting out to one thousand yards. Savage's shooting team has won a case full of trophies and medals as a result. The Model 12 is built the same way as Model 110s. The LE/Tactical 110 BA is a modular design that enables the operator to customize the rifle for mission specific needs. Try out a .338 Lapua Magnum.

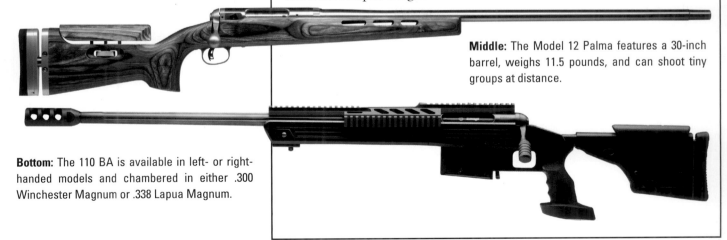

Middle: The Model 12 Palma features a 30-inch barrel, weighs 11.5 pounds, and can shoot tiny groups at distance.

Bottom: The 110 BA is available in left- or right-handed models and chambered in either .300 Winchester Magnum or .338 Lapua Magnum.

Colt M16

America's Black Rifle
Produced: 1959–Present

Fully automatic M16s have been used in the US Military since 1958, while civilian sales of semiautomatic versions, AR-15 rifles, began in 1963. Today it is perhaps the most copied rifle in the United States with dozens of manufacturers building countless numbers of variants that range from highly accurate competitions rifles and tactical models to varmint and big-game hunting rifles. The shooting public cannot get enough of what the Vietnam War–era grunts nicknamed the "Black Rifle."

The rifle's operating system is direct gas impingement, in which gas from a fired round travels from the barrel through a gas port, down a gas tube, and into a bolt carrier. The bolt carrier acts like a piston to eject the spent cartridge while a buffer spring in the stock pushes the bolt forward to chamber a new cartridge. The action is renowned for minimal recoil, especially when chambered for 5.56 NATO/.223 Remington ammo, the rifle's most common caliber. The modularity of the rifle allows upper and lower receivers to be easily swapped depending on the shooting scenario. AR-15s are also easily customized with the builder's imagination as the only limit. The rifle has been vilified in the anti-gun press and erroneously called an assault rifle, but the AR in AR-15 stands for ArmaLite Rifle. Shooters have found that the AR-15 is an excellent rifle capable of defending one's home, putting meat in the freezer, and competing in target shooting.

The rifle's design began to take shape in 1955–56 in Hollywood, California, at ArmaLite Corporation, a small machine shop that was purchased and made a subdivision of Fairchild Engine and Airplane Corporation. Eugene Stoner was hired as chief design engineer. ArmaLite's business plan was to design small arms to be sold or licensed. Stoner, Robert Fremont, and L. James Sullivan all worked on developing new small arms designs. The AR-10 was the predecessor to the M16. It fired a 7.62x51mm cartridge and was submitted to the US

Below: This is what the radical M16 looked like when first issued; it was chided for being "Made by Mattel," a toy manufacturer. Courtesy Springfield Armory National Historic Site.

Army's tests for a replacement for the M1 Garand. The AR-10 was unlike any rifle in the tests—non-reciprocating charging handle, hinged upper and lower components, select fire, gas-operated direct impingement system, lightweight aluminum receiver, synthetic stock, and aluminum/steel barrel, to name just a few unique design characteristics.

Above: The M16 was not issued with a cleaning kit, but that soon changed after rifles jammed in combat. Courtesy of Springfield Armory National Historic Site.

Right: A grunt in 'Nam carrying an M16; the weapon proved valuable after initial glitches. Courtesy of Springfield Armory National Historic Site.

Long story short (fill in the requisite political shenanigans and cover-ups as well as military changing and rechanging specifications), Colt demonstrated the AR-15 to General Curtis LeMay, Air Force Chief of Staff, on watermelons in Hagerstown, Maryland, in 1960. LeMay was convinced of the killing power of the rifle and its high velocity .22 caliber bullets. More political maneuverings ensued, but the M16 was issued to troops in South Vietnam in 1962. Initial reports stated the rifle was well received but a change in the rifle's cartridge powder proved to be disastrous. Rifles jammed, and GIs died. Cleaning kits and manuals were issued, and the rifle design was slightly tweaked. The M16 has since been modified over the years, and is now in the M4 model variants with a short and more maneuverable 14-inch barrel. Colt has been the only manufacturer to supply the M16 and its variants to the US Military, but that seems to be changing with Remington Defense named as a new contractor.

On the commercial or civilian side, the semiautomatic AR-15 has been banned, then the assault rifle ban was allowed to expire, and at times there have not been enough AR-15s on dealers' shelves. Many states still require post-ban configurations: welded muzzle brake, no bayonet lug, fixed buttstock, and ten-round magazines. Some states ban the rifle outright. In the 1990s the popularity of AR-15s surged with varmint hunters when manufacturers like Rock River Arms, DPMS, Daniel Defense, LaRue Tactical, Stag Arms, and others created extremely accurate coyote rifles. The AR-10 rifle in .308 Winchester makes the platform suitable for big game hunting.

Above: Like other military rifles of yore, the AR15 is now commonly used for hunting. Courtesy of National Sport Shooting Foundation.

Left: The M4 is the current M16 variant used in close- to medium-range combat in the streets of Iraq and Afghanistan. Courtesy of United States Army.

Specifications
CALIBER: 5.56x45mm NATO
BARREL LENGTH: 20 inches
OA LENGTH: 39.5 inches
WEIGHT: 7.18 pounds (unloaded)
STOCK: Polymer pistol grip, handguard
SIGHTS: Adjustable rear aperture/ winged adjustable front post
ACTION: Gas-operated direct impingement/rotating bolt, select fire
FINISH: Parkerized
CAPACITY: 20-, 30-round detachable box magazine

There is no doubt the political roil over "assault weapons" and the AR-15 will continue to be a flash point. In the meantime, firearms manufacturers and accessory manufacturers are building some of the best rifles and parts that have served our country since 1962.

Above: The semiautomatic AR-15 has replaced the pump shotgun as law enforcement's long gun. Courtesy of Colt Defense.

Right: The AR15 rifle is used by more competitors in the Service Rifle category than any other rifle. Courtesy of Civilian Marksmanship Program.

Comic Relief and Maintenance Procedures

In 1965 M16 rifles were issued to troops without cleaning supplies or even instructions on how to clean the rifles. In March of the same year, reports surfaced of grunts killed because their M16s had jammed. The cause was a change in the powder of the ammunition. The fix was a chrome-lined chamber, a recoil buffer modified for the ammo, and cleaning kits. Will Eisner's maintenance manual, written like a comic book, was also passed out to GIs. With the design changes and maintenance training, the reliability of the rifle increased and it gained acceptance and approval with the troops.

Left: Will Eisner wrote and illustrated "The M16A1 Rifle Operation and Preventive Maintenance" manual for the US Army.

Right: The gelatin block shows the effect of a 75-grain boat tail hollow point round. Courtesy of Hornady.

All About That Yaw

The .223 Remington/5.56x45mm cartridge was officially adopted by the US Army for use in the AR-15 platform in 1964. The round creates massive wounds, because it hits at high speed and tumbles or yaws in soft targets while transferring energy. Originally a 55-grain bullet was loaded in M193 ammo; in 2010 the bullet weight was changed to a 62-grain bullet in M855A1 ammo. Technically, the .223 Remington and the 5.56x45mm are slightly different, with 5.56 brass cases heavier than commercial .223 cases. Chambers and throats are also slightly different.

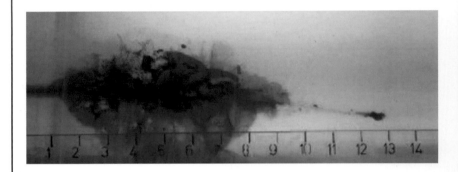

1960s

Mossberg 500

Econo Combo King
Production: 1960–Present

Mossberg needed a win in the late 1950s. They wanted a more modern-looking shotgun to compete with those made by Winchester, Remington, High Standard, and others. The 200 series shotgun was getting long in the tooth, so lead design engineer Carl Benson and his team set to work, and the result was the Model 500. Mossberg preferred to call it the 500 Shooting System, since the initial 12-gauge model offered a variety of interchangeable barrels. The 500 also featured an ambidextrous safety located at the top of the anodized aluminum receiver, single slide-bar, disconnecting trigger, damascened bolts, and solid steel-to-steel lock-up of the bolt to the barrel

The original design remained virtually unchanged for over thirty years. A characteristic of the Model 500 is that the bolt locks into a locking lug located on the top of the barrel—the solid steel-to-steel, bolt-to-barrel lock-up connection that Mossberg advertisements tout; this system does not rely on the receiver for any locking strength as some other pump-action shotguns do. The trigger assembly fieldstrips easily and quickly via one retaining pin, making the 500 easy to maintain. The aluminum receiver gives the 500 better balance and makes it lighter. Today only 12, 20, and .410 models are available, but in 1963 a 16-gauge version was offered that has long since been discontinued. Standard models have a magazine capacity of five 2-3/4-inch shells or four 3-inch shells. Some tactical models with an extended magazine tube have an 8+1 capacity.

Above: Mossberg 500 Turkey Thug is an inexpensive set-up for turkey hunting.

Top: The old school Classic model features blued steel, a wood stock, and a red ventilated recoil pad just like pump guns a few generations ago.

Specifications

GAUGE: 12, 16, 20, .410

BARREL LENGTH: 14 to 30 inches

OA LENGTH: 43.5 inches (24-in. barrel, 12-gauge)

WEIGHT: 7 lbs. (24-in. barrel, 12-gauge)

STOCK: Wood, Mossy Oak camo, or black synthetic

SIGHTS: HiViz or metal bead front, metal bead mid rib

ACTION: Pump-action

FINISH: Blue, nickel, Mossy Oak camo, Marinecote, or matte blue receiver/blued, camo, Marinecote, or matte blue barrel

CAPACITY: 5+1 (8+1 for some Tactical variants)

The charm of the inexpensive 500 is its versatility. Mossberg began selling combo kits consisting of a smoothbore bird barrel and a slug barrel with iron sights. A hunter could then set up his or her 500 for upland bird or whitetail deer hunting. Over the years, numerous configurations have been designed for law enforcement and military use. Between stocks, forends, and barrels, the 500 can be configured for nearly any scenario. Between the Model 500 and other pump-action shotgun models—505 Youth models, 510 Mini models, 535 ATS models, 835, 590, and others, Mossberg is the world's largest manufacturer of pump-action shotguns, besting the number two shotgun maker by 45 percent. Over ten million Model 500 pump-action shotguns have been produced. The Flex system introduced in 2014 enables users to quickly configure the 500 any way they want without the use of tools.

In my younger and more vulnerable years, before screw-in chokes were the norm and when money was tight, I purchased a Model 500 combo. It was inexpensive due to the pressed checkering on a hardwood stock. Tooling marks showed through the thin blued finish. That 500 combo allowed me to hunt grouse, pheasant, mallards, and whitetails. Changing from bird season to deer season was only a matter of changing out the barrel. I've shot thousands of rounds through that same 500 at clay targets—sporting clays, skeet, and trap—and won a few games of Annie Oakley with it; it has never failed me. No, it's not fancy, but it sure does work.

Above: Just in case there is a zombie hoard roaming the countryside, a Model 500 with a chainsaw forend can help mow down the undead.

Above: The FLEX System gives the over-fifty-year-old design of the Model 500 a new level of versatility unlike any other pump gun manufacturer.

Military and LE Mossbergs

The Model 590 series is based on the Model 500 pump shotgun. Mossberg asserts the Model 500 was the only shotgun that met US Army mil-spec 3443E. The spec has since been revised. Section 3.10.12 of MIL-S-3443G added a requirement that the trigger guard be made of metal and be able to withstand a static load of 220 pounds applied to the trigger guard bow. In layman's terms, the trigger guard should have sufficient strength to take a blow without deforming and jamming the trigger mechanism. Mossberg updated the Model 590 to the 590A1, which has a metal trigger guard and other updated modifications like a barrel lug that slips over the magazine tube and is secured with a magazine cap, aluminum safety button, and thicker barrel walls. The steel components are also phosphate-coated. Model 590A1s have a polymer trigger group. The Navy uses the 590A1s. The Connecticut State Police and Texas Dept. of Public Safety are just two examples of LE agencies that rely on Mossbergs. The Texas training shotguns have some fifteen thousand rounds through them and they are still running strong.

Remington Model 700

Three Rings of Steel
Produced: 1962–Present

The Model 700 and the 7mm Remington Magnum go back to 1962. John F. Kennedy was in his second year in the White House. Coca-Cola was ten cents, it only came in a tall, heavy glass bottle, and you needed a bottle opener to open it. And Winchester and Remington were locked in a marketing rivalry. Winchester was riding the wave of enthusiasm over their recent .264 Winchester Magnum, which hit dealers' shelves in 1953. It was a fast cartridge that left the .270 Win and .30-06 in the dust. Remington needed a win.

Below: The Model 700 BDL has old-school looks with the newest Remington innovations.

When tailfins on cars were still common, Remington debuted a bolt-action rifle in a new magnum caliber, 7mm Remington Magnum. It would be a cliché to say the rest is history, but ever since the Model 700 has been a benchmark in rifle design and the 7mm Rem Mag cartridge has been one of the most popular cartridges ever. More than five million different model 700s have been built since in forty calibers ranging from the .17 Rem to the .458 Win Mag. That makes over nine hundred models type/caliber combinations. It helped at the time that Winchester decided to redesign their Model 70 into a push-feed rifle, turning off loyal Winchester customers.

Merle "Mike" Walker and Remington's design crew in the 1940s was tasked with designing a rifle that was more economical to manufacture than the Model 721 and Model 722. Usually when the goal is to cut costs, that means

Below: With the bolt retracted, the innermost ring of steel can be seen in the bolt face on the Model 700.

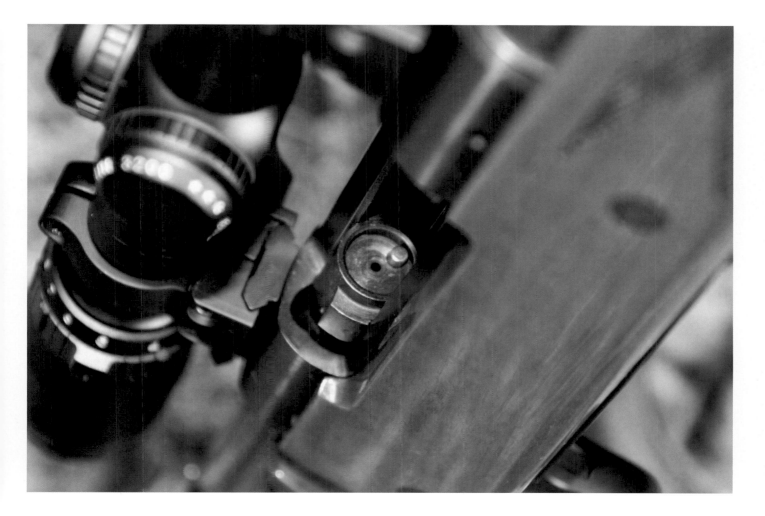

cheapening the product. In the case of the Model 700, the rifle was easier and simpler to manufacture and the design was exceptionally strong. Remington marketing material at the time touted "three rings of steel" that provided strength and accuracy. The three rings of steel are three key components of the Model 700. The first is the bolt face, which is recessed to enclose the base of the cartridge. The second ring is the chamber end of the barrel, which surrounds the bolt face. The third ring is the front receiver ring, which in turn surrounds the chamber end of the barrel.

The Model 700 utilizes a push-feed bolt with two forward lugs; the bolt handle acts as a rear lug. The extractor is set within the bolt face as is the ejector, which is a plunger type. The action is available in three sizes; short for .308 size cartridges, standard for .30-06 length rounds, and long for magnum-sized rounds. The US government purchases the Model 700 from Remington Defense as the sniper dedicated M24. Countless custom rifle makers build rifles using the Model 700 as a platform.

I have a Model 700 BDL, which is about as old school looking as you can get in a Model 700. The walnut stock features a high Monte Carlo cheekpiece for right-handed shooters, skipline pattern checkering, and a dark wood end cap. The stock's finish is so glossy you can shave in the reflection. The white spacer between the stock and the recoil pad was how gunmakers once dressed up rifles, but by today's standards of matte steel and synthetic stocks, the spacer looks like white socks with a tuxedo. Simply, it looks like a 1960s-era rifle. The bluing is glossy and deep. A hinged floorplate is standard on the BDL. The BDL's 24-inch barrel is slightly tapered and sports what may seem strange to current shooters: open sights. The rear is ramp style with easily read graduation marks for elevation and windage. The front sight consists of a hooded ramp. Open sights on modern bolt-action rifles are as rare today as tailfins on a car. The twist rate is 9-1/4:1 for 7mm Rem Mag.

The X-Mark Pro Trigger has been adorning Model 700s since 2009. The trigger is adjustable just in case the factory setting of 3-1/2 pounds does not suit your needs. The trigger can be adjusted up or down two pounds from the factory setting using a common hex wrench. On the BDL, the trigger broke crisply at 3 pounds 10 ounces. No need to adjust. Bolt work was typical Remington and at first was sticky but after a few strokes it

Opposite Page: The Remington Model 700 touted its "out-of-the-box" accuracy in an ad from the 1980s.

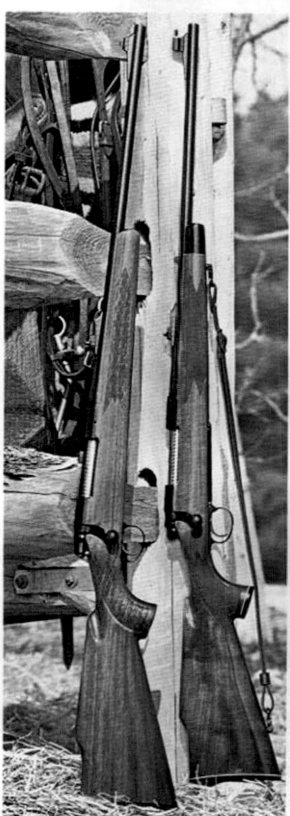

The initial ADL has since been eclipsed with numerous styles, like the Model 700 Sendero SF II featuring a heavy fluted 26-inch barrel, full-length aluminum bedding, and synthetic stock with finger grooves and palm swells. The Model 700 VL SS Thumbhole has a 26-inch heavy contour barrel and laminated thumbhole stock. The Model 700 SPS Tactical AAC-SD features a 20-inch heavy barrel with a threaded muzzle.

smoothed up. The sides of the bolt now are checkered and shaft of the bolt is nicely jeweled.

Since 1962 the Model 700 has been wildly popular with hunters, and competitive shooters. That's not bad for over a half a century.

Remington's Big Seven: Long Range Punch

The 7mm Remington Magnum is a relatively new pup compared to cartridges like the .30-06 and .270 Win., which debuted in 1906 and 1925, respectively. Introduced in 1962, the 7mm Rem. Mag. was designed to compete with the old-timers. According to the Boone and Crocket Club, the .30-06 and the 7mm Rem. Mag. tied in popularity. What B&C record holders know is what a lot of big game hunters have known since the early 1960s: the 7mm Rem. Mag. shoots as flat as the .270 Win. and has the same power as the .30-06, and it does this using the same size action as the .270 and .30-06. The 7mm Rem Mag. shines at long ranges found in the western United States and the plains of Africa. The 7mm Rem. Mag. is a belted cartridge that carries the same DNA as the .300 H&H and .375 H&H Magnums. Belted cartridges have a belt around the base of the cartridge that allows the cartridge to headspace on the belt. The .270 and .30-06 headspace on the cartridge case shoulder. Belted cartridges also ensure better extraction as the rim is exposed. Holland & Holland (H&H) originally designed the belted case for their large caliber, dangerous–game rounds and ever since magnum cartridges and belted cartridges have become synonymous.

When the 7mm Rem. Mag. debuted, the hot cartridge at the time was the .264 Winchester. Big Seven's presence caused the .264 Win.'s popularity to fizzle as it took on the .30-06 and .270 head to head. On paper and in the field the 7mm Rem. Mag. offers better ballistics. The 7mm bullet is slipperier in the air than a .30 caliber bullet, meaning 7mm bullets have a better BC (ballistic coefficient). The 7mm Rem. Mag.'s sweet spot with bullet weights is in the range 140 to 160 grains and with barrel lengths between 24 and 26 inches. Shorter barrels suck the velocity out of the 7mm Rem. Mag. not allowing bullets to achieve full velocity. With similar rifle weights and bullet weight/velocities the

---

Specifications

CALIBER: .17 Rem Fireball, .204 Ruger, .220 Swift, .22-250, .243 Win., .25-06, .257 Wby. Mag., .260 Rem., .264 Win. Mag., .270 Win., .270 WSM, .280 Rem., 7mm-08, 7mm Rem. Mag., 7mm Rem. Ultra Mag., .30-06, .300 Win. Mag., .300 WSM, .308 Win., .300 Rem. Ultra Mag., .338 Win. Mag., .338 Rem. Ultra Mag., .35 Whelan, .375 Rem. Ultra Mag., .375 H&H Magnum, .416 Rem. Mag., .416 Rigby, .458 Win. Mag., .470 Capstick

BARREL LENGTH: 20, 22, 24, and 26 inches (depending on caliber/model)

WEIGHT: 9 pounds (average depending on caliber/barrel length)

STOCK: Checkered wood or polymer

SIGHTS: Adjustable rear/ramp post front

ACTION: Bolt, push feed, two-lug

FINISH: Blued or stainless

CAPACITY: 3, 4, 5, and 6 internal box (standard)

Below: A 7mm Remington Magnum with a 150-grain Core-Lokt is flanked on the left by a Remington .270 Winchester with a 130-grain Core-Lokt and on the right a Remington .30-06 with a 168-grain Core-Lokt Ultra Bonded PSP.

7mm Rem. Mag. has on average 15 percent more recoil than the .30-06. On the plus side the Big Seven's recoil is much tamer than other magnums, like the .300 Win. Mag. and .338 Win. Mag. It is not a caliber for new shooters, but if that is the only rifle available in deer camp, try stoking it with Remington's Managed Recoil cartridges that offer less kick.

M24 Sniper Weapon System

When the US Army spec'd out a dedicated sniper rifle, they started with the commercial Model 700 action platform. The M24 SWS (Sniper Weapon System) was adopted by the Army in 1988 and includes the rifle and accessories, like a Leupold scope, tools, spares, Harris bipod, and sling. The M24 starts with a long-action Model 700 receiver, since the rifle was originally going to use .30–06 Springfield ammunition then changed to shorter 7.62x51mm NATO (.308 Winchester) ammo (the bolt length remained the same). The thought was the rifle could be retrofitted in a caliber the same length as the .30-06, such as the .300 Winchester Magnum. Some fifteen thousand M24s have been built by Remington Arms to US Army specifications.

Top: The US Army designed the M24 starting with the Model 700 to be a dedicated sniper rifle and was adopted by the Army in 1988. Courtesy Remington Defense.

Left: Military operators have come to appreciate the M24 as a reliable rifle with an effective range to 800 meters. Courtesy Remington Defense.

Remington Model 1100

Soft Shooter
Production: 1963–Present

Semiautomatic shotguns were not new in the early 1960s. Browning had designed a recoil-operated shotgun in 1902. Using the burning gases from a fired shell to operate a shotgun's mechanism was still out of reach for most manufacturers. They built some autoloaders, but the reliability was spotty and shooters needed to make adjustments depending on the shells fired. Recoil-operated guns used friction rings, and guns like those made by High Standard had a selector that a user switched depending on the shell. The Remington 1100 changed all of that. One could easily argue the new design was revolutionary. Remington's first attempts at producing a gas-operated shotgun were the Model 58 and Sportsman 58, which were built from 1956 to 1963. The Model 58 was an attempt. (Underscore attempt.) Other manufacturers like High Standard had been producing gas-operated semiautomatic shotguns like the Supermatic since 1960. In 1963 when Remington came out with the Model 1100, the successor to the Model 58, shotgun shooting was transformed.

The Model 1100 was designed by Wayne Leek and R. Kelley using analogue computers with miles of wire, oscilloscopes, and tubes—enough to fill a room.

Almost immediately, it became the most popular gas-operated semiautomatic shotgun in America for one major reason—soft recoil. The Remington was also reliable and required none of the user adjustments to low-brass or high-brass shells like previous models. In 1978, an 1100 fired twenty-four thousand rounds before it malfunctioned, and it was not cleaned during all those rounds.

The 1100 took the "kick" out of shooting a 12-gauge, or any gauge for that matter. The measured amount of reduced recoil was about 40 percent less than other semiautomatic shotguns of the time. The 1100's system operates by bleeding off the expanding gases of a fired shell through ports in the barrel near the end of the forend. The gases then drive a sleeve around the magazine tube that connects to the bolt carrier group via action bars. What was novel about the design at the time was the system was self-compensating. Nearly any 2-3/4-inch shell can be fired in the shotguns without the operator having to make any adjustments on the gun. Another design feature of the Model 1100 is the carrier release is positioned near the magazine loading port so shells can easily be fed into the tube magazine and bolt released with minimal hand movement. Most other gas-operated semiautomatic shotguns locate the carrier release on the side of the receiver. Barrels could also be interchanged quickly and easily so one could chase pheasant in the morning then swap the smoothbore barrel for a rifled slug barrel and lay in wait for a buck in a tree stand. The features we shooters and hunters take for granted in today's semiautomatic shotgun were introduced with the 1100. Over four million 1100s have been built and for good reason: shooters love them.

Everyone has an 1100 story. The first 1100 I fired was well-used. It had been handed down from a dad to his eldest son to the next oldest son. There was hardly any bluing left on the receiver and the finish was flaking off the stock. I could hit anything tossed up in the air that day. I'll bet that 1100 is still working today.

Specifications	
GAUGE: 12, 16, 20, 28, .410	
BARREL LENGTH: 18 to 30 inches	
OA LENGTH: 45.6 inches (24-in. barrel) to 49.6 inches (28-in. barrel)	
WEIGHT: 8 lbs. (28-in. barrel, 12-gauge)	
STOCK: Glossy walnut or synthetic	
SIGHTS: HiViz or metal bead front, metal bead mid rib	
ACTION: Gas-operated, semiautomatic	
FINISH: Blued, nickel or matte black receiver/blued or matte black barrel	
CAPACITY: 4+1 (3+1 for Special Field 12 and 20 gauge models and .410 using 3-in. shells)	

Remington 11-87: Juiced Up 1100

The 11-87 was introduced in 1987 at a time when Beretta's A303 semiauto shotguns were gaining traction with shooters and hunters. The 11-87 is essentially an 1100, but the 11-87 will shoot all 2-3/4-inch and 3-inch loads interchangeably, unlike the 1100.

Ruger 10/22

Tin Can Buster and Squirrel Hunter
Produced: 1964–Present

The 10/22 is an iconic American rimfire rifle with a slick rotary magazine. Some five million have been manufactured since introduced in 1964. The 10/22 is a fun plinker and small-game getter. It is also highly customizable, and since it is an easy rifle to work on, many shooters trick out their 10/22 to suit their shooting situation or their personality. After-market triggers, barrels, and stocks can completely transform the factory 10/22 into a custom shooting machine.

Bill Ruger and Harry Sefried both designed the rifle. The 10/22 was designed as a full-size rimfire rifle. It uses a simple blow back mechanism. When fired, the bolt travels rearward until it hits the bolt stop pin. At that point the bolt is delayed enough for the empty case to eject and a new round to feed through the magazine. It is a marvelously simple design. The magazine itself is quite unique for a rimfire, as it features a rotor that separates cartridges and provides reliable feeding. Loading the magazines is easy too. The reliability and the ease of use is what make the Ruger 10/22 stand out from the crowd of other .22 LR rifles.

Left: The novelty and reliability of the rotary magazine was stressed in early Ruger 10/22 ads.

Below: The Standard Carbine model has been virtually unchanged since it was introduced in 1964.

Get High Power Quality with the
RUGER® 10/22 Carbine

There is no finer 22 rimfire than a Ruger 10/22 autoloading Carbine.

The 10/22 Carbine is built to high power rifle quality throughout, *with everything made better than it needs to be.*

10/22 Carbine with Sporter stock

Construction of the 10/22 Carbine is exceptionally rugged and follows the Ruger design practice of building a firearm from integrated sub-assemblies. For example, the trigger housing assembly contains the entire ignition system, which employs a high-speed swinging hammer to insure the shortest possible lock time. The barrel is assembled to the receiver by a unique dual-screw dovetail system that provides unusual rigidity and strength — and accounts, in part, for the superb accuracy of the 10/22.

Full use is made of modern materials whenever they provide unique advantages and yet the finest of steel and wood remain whenever required by function or tradition. This latter

is most noticeable in the 10/22 Carbine stock which is precision machined from a solid block of American Walnut.

Accurate, Reliable, Rugged, Fast Handling, Light, Compact and priced to be an Exceptional Value . . . the Ruger 10/22 Carbine is a unique pleasure to own.

Specifications:

Caliber: .22 long rifle, high-speed or standard velocity loads. Barrel: 18½" length. Weight: 5 pounds. Overall Length: 37". Sights: 1⁄16" gold bead front. Single folding leaf rear. Receiver drilled and tapped for scope blocks or tip-off mount adapter. Magazine: 10-shot capacity. Trigger: Curved finger surface, 3⁄8" wide. Safety: Sliding cross-button type. Safety locks both sear and hammer and cannot be put in safe position unless gun is cocked. Stocks: Solid American walnut, oil finished. Available in two styles: The Standard Carbine and The Sporter. Finish: Polished all over and blued or anodized. Prices: 10/22 Standard Carbine — $54.50. 10/22 Sporter — $64.50.

UNIQUE 10-SHOT ROTARY MAGAZINE. Simple and rugged. Retaining lips and ramps that guide the cartridge are solid steel alloy that won't bend or deform. As a result, feeding malfunctions are eliminated. Magazine fits smoothly within the configuration of the 10/22 Carbine and is released by the latch located behind the magazine.

Best quality open sights as used on high power rifles. The rear sight is adjustable for elevation and windage and folds down to permit use of a low mounted scope.

STURM, RUGER
AND COMPANY, INCORPORATED
Southport, Connecticut 06490 U.S.A.

ALL RUGER FIREARMS ARE DESIGNED AND MANUFACTURED IN OUR OWN FACTORIES IN THE UNITED STATES OF AMERICA.

Marlin Model 60

Introduced in 1960, the Model 60 is also a very popular rimfire rifle featuring Marlin's micro-groove barrel rifling that uses sixteen small lands and grooves to increase accuracy by decreasing the deformation of bullets as they travel down the barrel. Typical rifling employs four, six, or eight grooves. Economically priced, the Model 60 easily allows for mounting optics, and with a Monte Carlo hardwood stock it is no wonder many young shooters cut their teeth on the Model 60.

Above: The Marlin Model 60 is another well-liked and reliable .22 rimfire autoloader.

Heavy Metal

The Ruger 10/22 Target variant features a heavy tapered hammer-forged barrel with a spiral design. The two-stage trigger has a short take up first stage, then the second stage is a crisp pull with no creep or over travel. I've plinked with the model and I think it is my favorite 10/22.

Left: The heavy barrel of the 10/22 Target ensures great accuracy and no felt recoil.

Plastic Fantastic

Well before the Marlin Model 60 or the Ruger 10/22, Remington debuted a .22 rimfire rifle in 1959 called the Nylon 66 that made use of a synthetic stock and receiver, which was odd for the day as well as cutting edge in material technology for rifles. It was one of the first mass-produced rifles to use a synthetic stock, which was made of Nylon Zytel-101, DuPont material, and held fourteen rounds in a tubular magazine inside the stock. Over one million Nylon 66 models were produced until production stopped in 1989. Today synthetic stocks are common.

Specifications

CALIBER: .22 LR

BARREL LENGTH: 16.6, 18.5, and 20 inches (depending on model)

WEIGHT: 5 pounds (Carbine variant with 20-in. barrel)

STOCK: Smooth hardwood (standard) or polymer

SIGHTS: Adjustable notched rear/ ramp post front; optic ready

ACTION: Blow back, semiautomatic

FINISH: Blued or stainless

CAPACITY: Detachable 10-round rotary magazine

Opposite Page: The 10/22 is compact, with no recoil, and absolutely reliable.

Ruger No.1

Opposite page: The Ruger No.1 evoked the great sporting tradition of stalking and killing game with one well-placed shot.

Below: Bill Ruger, no doubt posing, but perhaps pondering the design details of a new gun on his drawing board.

Specifications

CALIBER: .204 Ruger, .22 Hornet, .218 Bee, .222 Remington, .223 Remington, .22 PPC, .22-250 Remington, .220 Swift, 6mm PPC, 6 mm Remington, .243 Winchester, .257 Roberts, .25-06 Remington, .264 Winchester Magnum, .270 Winchester, .270 Weatherby Magnum, 6.5mm Remington, 6.5x55mm, 7x57mm, 7mm-08, .280 Remington, 7 mm Remington Magnum, 7 mm STW, .308 Winchester, .30-30 Winchester, .30-40 Krag, .30-06 Springfield, .303 British, .300 Winchester Magnum, .300 H&H Magnum, .300 Weatherby Magnum, .338 Winchester Magnum, .357 Magnum, .375 H&H Magnum, .375 Ruger, .38-55 Winchester, .404 Jeffery, .405 Winchester, .416 Remington Magnum, .416 Ruger, .416 Rigby, .45-70 Government, .460 S&W Magnum, .458 Winchester Magnum, .458 Lott, 9.3 x 74R or .450/400 Nitro Express

The American Single-Shot Redux
Produced: 1966–Present

Bill Ruger loved old guns, and he also liked to reengineer them to make them better. At a time when a single-shot rifle was the last thing on anyone's mind, Ruger introduced the single-shot No. 1. The shooting public was smitten and it made perfect sense in hindsight. After all, our country had cut its teeth on single-shot rifles a century earlier with the likes of Sharps, Remington, Ballard, Maynard, Stevens, and Winchester 1885 single-shot rifles.

Single Shot Rifle

A return to a great sporting tradition.

Why have we built a single-shot in this day of self-loaders and repeaters? Today's reason for the single-shot is oddly analogous to that which inspired the great single-shot rifles of the 1870's: To produce a more efficient long-range rifle. In the '70's, the single-shot was the most powerful type because it could digest outsized cartridges. Today, the Ruger Single-Shot can have a 4½" longer barrel than a comparable bolt-action rifle of the same overall length. Accordingly, the Ruger Single-Shot obtains greatly increased velocity from modern magnum cartridges. In addition to this significant ballistic advantage, the Ruger No. 1 Single-Shot combines handsome lines and perfect balance with the luxury of a closely fitted action — a rifle to appeal to the connoisseur.

Beyond these physical advantages is the challenge of the single shot — which puts to a true test the skill and marksmanship of the hunter who works hard stalking, loves life in the open, and never hunts in a way that takes unfair advantage of the game.

The under-lever, falling-block action of the No. 1 Single-Shot is engineered to modern standards of strength and performance. You will find the rifle finished to a degree of perfection that is unsurpassed by the best of old or modern firearms. Stock and forearm are genuine American walnut, individually hand fitted and hand checkered, and then hand rubbed to a glowing oil finish. Two forearm styles are available: a short, slim type in the classic style of Alexander Henry — and a longer semi-beavertail style.

The rifle may be purchased in a variety of hunting, varmint, and target configurations, with forearm and sighting equipment options. It is chambered for a growing list of almost all modern cartridges, and a few obsolete ones.

Return to one of the great traditions of sport with the ageless grace of the Ruger No. 1 Single-Shot rifle. *Our comprehensive brochure awaits your inquiry.*

STURM, RUGER & Company, Inc.
SOUTHPORT, CONNECTICUT, U.S.A.

BARREL LENGTH: 22, 24, and 26 inches (depending on caliber/model)

WEIGHT: 7 pounds (average depending on caliber/barrel length)

STOCK: Checkered walnut

SIGHTS: Adjustable rear/ramp post front or optic ready

ACTION: Farquharson-style hammerless falling block

FINISH: Blued or stainless

CAPACITY: Single-shot

The falling block action of the Ruger No.1 is a modified version of the English Farquharson-style action with internal hammer. A lever that locks into the trigger guard is pressed down to drop the massive stainless steel block, expose the rifle's chamber to load or unload a cartridge, and cock the hammer. It is an exceptionally strong action that Ruger has chambered in some fifty different calibers over the years. The wood on the rifle is also exceptional with three types of forearms offered: a unique Alexander-Henry, a Beavertail for varmint-chambered rifles, and a full-length Mannlicher style.

Because of the action style, the length of the rifle's receiver is reduced so the overall length is less than a bolt-action with the same barrel length. The action is also thin, so it carries easy. When it comes time to shoot, the ambidextrous thumb safety is conveniently placed under the shooter's thumb. My current No.1 is an International variant with a full Mannlicher stock and chambered in 7x57mm, a sweet carrying and shooting rifle for whitetails.

The No.1 rifles from Ruger are unique, sophisticated, and harken back to a time when single-shot big bores were the ultimate hunting rifles.

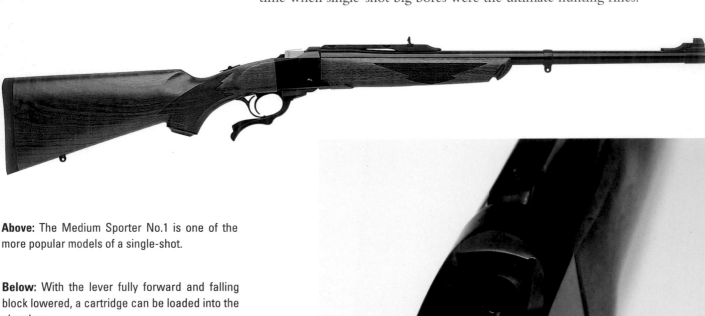

Above: The Medium Sporter No.1 is one of the more popular models of a single-shot.

Below: With the lever fully forward and falling block lowered, a cartridge can be loaded into the chamber.

Above: The Sharps Model 1874 (top), Winchester Model 1885 High Wall (middle), and Remington Rolling Block (bottom) were all single-shot big bore rifles used at the end of the nineteenth century for hunting and long-range target shooting.

Thompson-Center Contender

Specifications

CALIBER: .17 HMR, .22 LR, .204 Ruger, .223 Remington, 6.8 Remington, 7-30 Waters, .30-30 Winchester, .375 Winchester, .44 Magnum, .45 Long Colt, .45-70 Government

BARREL LENGTH: 6, 8.75, 10, 12, 14, 16, and 21 inches

WEIGHT: 43 ounces (10-in. barrel)

STOCK: Smooth walnut

SIGHTS: Adjustable rear/ramp post front, optic ready

ACTION: Break-action, exposed hammer

FINISH: Blued or stainless

CAPACITY: Single-shot

40 Barrel Choices and Counting
Produced: 1967–Present

The Contender and the newer second generation Contender G2 model pistol—or rifles or muzzleloaders—allow a hunter to swap barrels in numerous calibers—rimfire or centerfire—and reconfigure the frame with a stock or pistol grip to be a rifle or pistol respectively. A TC Contender G2 has a variety of possible configurations so you can go from hunting squirrels to turkeys to elk.

Warren Center developed the Contender in his basement, then partnered with the K.W. Thompson Tool Company to build the pistol. The single-shot pistol uses a break action where the trigger guard is pulled back to open the action for loading and unloading. The hammer is then cocked back to fire the pistol. The barrel is attached to the frame via a large hinge pin. By simply taking off the forend, the pin can be removed and another barrel can be swapped out. The G2 model replaced the Contender in 2002, and the Encore is latest generation with the same capabilities as the Contender and G2 and the added ability to use muzzleloading rifles.

Below: This G2 is set up as a rifle with long barrel, buttstock, and optic. Courtesy Smith & Wesson Corp.

There is something about these TC guns that tickle the frugal Yankee in me. A versatile gun with many options.

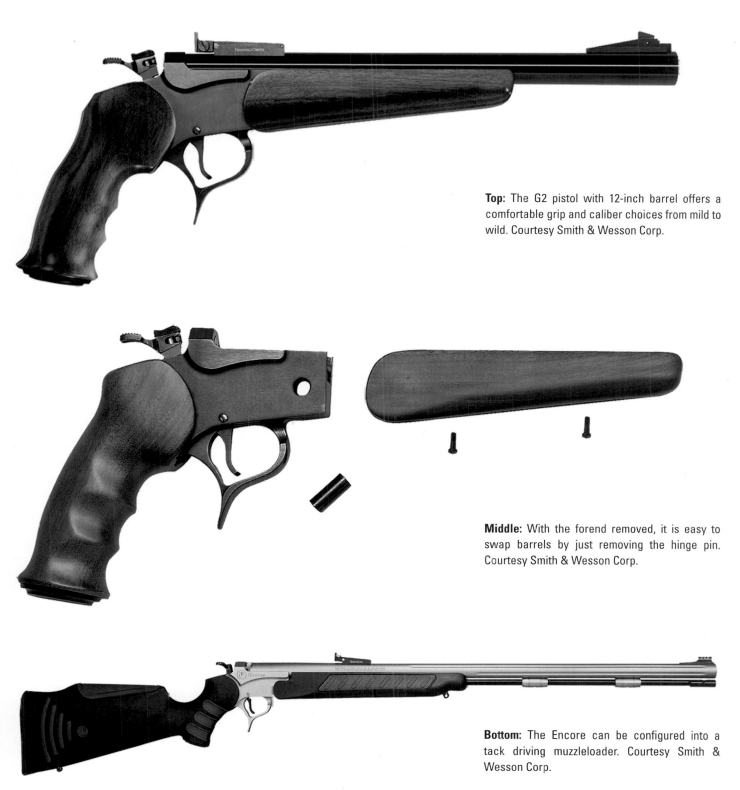

Top: The G2 pistol with 12-inch barrel offers a comfortable grip and caliber choices from mild to wild. Courtesy Smith & Wesson Corp.

Middle: With the forend removed, it is easy to swap barrels by just removing the hinge pin. Courtesy Smith & Wesson Corp.

Bottom: The Encore can be configured into a tack driving muzzleloader. Courtesy Smith & Wesson Corp.

Browning BT-99

Specifications
GAUGE: 12
BARREL LENGTH: 32 inches
WEIGHT: 8.1 pounds
STOCK: Checkered black walnut
SIGHTS: Ivory front bead
ACTION: Break-action
FINISH: Satin blued
CAPACITY: Single-shot

How Trap Should Be Played
Produced: 1969–Present

Not long after the Browning BT-99 was introduced it became wildly popular and revered for its simplicity, durability, and clay-target-busting performance on the trap field. You can literally shoot the BT-99 until your shoulder is black and blue and it will continue to shoot. It is a tough competitor.

As a dedicated trapshooting gun, the BT-99 is a single-shot that uses a boxlock action. The chambers are chromed to resist fouling from all those thousands of rounds you'll put through it. Newer models have Vector Pro forcing cones to minimize shot deformation and maximize shot patterns. Think consistency and density. Barrel lengths are typically 32 inches, but stock configurations and finish choices are numerous.

Above: The Conventional BT-99 offers a reliable entry-level trap gun that can compete out of the box.

Above: High grade models like this BT-99 Golden Clays has a fully adjustable stock.

Perazzi MX8

Top Gun Competitor
Produced: 1968–Present

The Perazzi MX series of shotguns are born competitors. In 1968 Perazzi shotguns started gaining notice as a result of their winning records. Elio Matarelli won Olympic gold at the 1968 games. Perazzis are designed to perform and are made to last, especially in grueling competition and lifetimes of practice. If winning competitions and durability don't set Perazzis apart from the competition, the modular aspect of the guns is impressive. The trigger group drops out and can be swapped out for, say, selective or non-selective trigger systems. The stock, too, is made to be easily removed.

The MX8 starts with a forged steel low-profile receiver. Barrel pivots on rugged pins and the lock-up between barrel and receiver is tight and strong. Even after thousands of fired rounds a Perazzi does not work loose. The receiver is slightly wider than other competition guns due to the removable trigger group.

What also sets a Perazzi apart from its competitors is price. They are handcrafted guns and are insanely expensive, but it is a small cost to have one of the best competition shotguns available.

Specifications
GAUGE: 410, 28, 20, or 12 (3-in. chamber)
BARREL LENGTH: 29.5, 30.75, or 31.75 inches
WEIGHT: 8.46 lbs.
STOCK: Walnut, numerous grades
FRONT SIGHT: Fiber optic
ACTION: Break action
FINISH: Blued
CAPACITY: 2

Above: The MX8 Vintage is similar to what the 12-gauge over-and-under looked like back in the late 1960s.

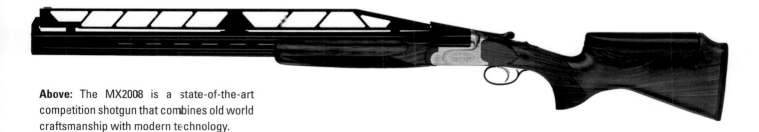

Above: The MX2008 is a state-of-the-art competition shotgun that combines old world craftsmanship with modern technology.

1970s–1990s

Browning Citori

America's Reigning Over-and-Under
Produced: 1973–Present

The story of the Citori actually begins with the Browning Superposed. The popularity of over-and-under shotguns rose as hammerless shotguns were first manufactured and over-and-under guns started to replace side-by-side guns. The Superposed design took shape from about 1922 through 1931. It was John Browning's last firearm design, and when he died in 1926, his son Val Browning took over. The original production started in 1931 in Belgium with only a 12-gauge model available. To American sportsmen the Superposed was revolutionary, since it featured innovations like a selective trigger, ventilated rib, and automatic ejectors. Today most shooters expect these features in an over-and-under. The Browning firearm company's reputation as a shotgun manufacturer was built with the Superposed as one of the cornerstones. It was durable and achieved a legendary status as an American shotgun. Even during the Great Depression and World War II the Superposed sold well. It also became the steel and wood canvas of engravers, with luxury Diana and gold-inlayed Midas models.

As is the case with many great firearm designs, the Superposed was expensive to manufacture, so Browning introduced the Japanese-manufactured Citori in 1973 as an economical and affordable version of the Superposed. Though the shooting and hunting public may have been skeptical of an inexpensive Superposed, the Citori has proven to be an extremely popular shotgun for generations of trap, skeet, and sporting clay shooters as well as waterfowl and upland bird hunters. In fact, it is one of the bestselling over-and-under shotguns in the world.

The Citori's reputation as a durable shotgun begins with the receiver, which is machined from solid steel. The actions are hand-fitted, and like the Superposed, the barrels of the Citori pivot on a full-length hinge pin.

Introducing the Browning Citori trap gun

A new high post rib, Browning workmanship and available extra barrels make it your best buy in an over/under trap gun.

Since its introduction three years ago, the Browning Citori has earned a reputation as a durable, dependable double. Now it's available with the extras top competition trap shooters have been asking for. And at a price you can afford. $517.50*

High Post Floating Vent Rib. This high rib design acts as a highway — your eyes travel quickly to the target. The under surface of the rib is dovetailed, allowing it to "float" on the posts. This rib won't bind a hot barrel and change your point of impact. The barrel can expand naturally. This rib's high post configuration raises the sighting plane in relation to the gun's center of gravity. The center of impact on your shoulder is lowered, lessening felt recoil and muzzle jump. Add the front and center ivory sight beads atop a fine matted sighting plane, and you have today's best target rib. A lesser rib may cost you a bird.

Extra Barrels. You can order your Citori trap gun with an extra set of barrels. Shoot 32" barrels in handicap events. And shorter, faster-pointing 30" barrels in doubles and 16 yard events. You can choose either barrel set with Full-Full, Imp. Mod.-Full or Mod.-Full chokes. You can shoot barrels and chokes specialized for the event and still get the same fit and trigger pull in all events. When you order your Citori with extra barrels, the set comes with a tough, fitted luggage case.

Built-to-last Craftsmanship. You want your trap gun to look as good as it shoots. The Citori does. Its select, tight grained walnut stock and forearm are hand checkered 20 lines to the inch. All the Citori's exterior metal parts are deeply polished and blued.

Extra Barrels in Cases.

High Post Floating Rib.

Cut Checkered Walnut.

The trigger is gold plated. Swing the new Citori trap gun at your Browning Dealer's. You'll see why it's your best buy in an over/under trap gun. *suggested retail price*

BROWNING
America's Great Trap Guns.
Copyright © Browning 1977

Full width length tapered locking bolt with larger locking surfaces and the full width hinge pin create a tight lockup and resist wear. Hammer ejectors provide more positive shell ejection than competitive brands. The top opening lever is crisp and sharp and will perform for tens of thousands of rounds.

Above: Citori Feather Lightning.

Specifications

CALIBER: 410, 28, 20, or 12 (3-inch chamber)

BARREL LENGTH: 26, 28, and 30 inches

OVERALL LENGTH: 43 inches to 47 inches

WEIGHT: 6.6 pounds to 8.4 pounds

STOCK: Walnut, numerous grades

FRONT SIGHT: Silver bead or HiViz Pro-Comp

ACTION: Break-action

FINISH: Blued, numerous finish options

CAPACITY: 2

The safety does not automatically engage when the action is open. Move the safety left or right to choose which barrel—top or bottom—will fire first with the single selective triggers. Inertia trigger systems were historically used to prevent a shooter from inadvertently pulling the trigger and firing the second barrel due to the recoil of the first shot. A shooter does not notice the time it takes to reset the trigger, as it is nearly indiscernible. The Citori 725 Sporting Clay and Trap models feature a mechanical trigger that automatically switches from one barrel to other. The 725's trigger reduces trigger take up, has a crisp break and shorter over travel.

Over the years design modifications to the Citori line can be divided into distinct types that are easily identified by receiver shape and serial number designation. The first Citoris are referred to as pre-Type 1 and were made from 1973 through 1976; the receivers on these shotguns have no engraving. Type 1 models were manufactured in 1977 only, have a slanted receiver, and contain the letter designation RR within the serial number. Type 2, or straight receiver, refers to shotguns manufactured between 1978 and 1982; the serial number will contain one of the following letter designations: RP, RN, PM, PZ, or PY. These types closely resemble the Superposed. Type 3, or radius receiver/long tang trigger guard models, refer to guns built from 1983 up through the present. The bottom edge of the receiver is radiused. The Type 3, or radius receiver/long tang trigger guard, is found on all Field and Target models produced since 1994. The serial number for all Citoris is located under the top lever.

Left: Citori XT Trap.

The Browning Citori also combines beauty and durability with various grades of finish from Grade 1, which features a checkered American Walnut stock and lightly engraved blued receiver, to Grade V with Grade IV/V featuring walnut wood and deep relief engraving. Compared to some Italian brands, the Citori has a heavier, some would say clunkier, action that is taller than a Beretta 680 series or a DT10 or DT11.

I have an old Citori 425 Sporting Clays model that I bought used. The stock was scratched, and that was just as well. The Citori is made to be used and used often. Keep the Midas version under a glass case to fawn over. I have used it for sporting clays, as well as skeet and trap. I'm frugal, so I use it to chase pheasant behind pointers. No matter how many hundreds of rounds I've fired through the Citori, it still locks up tight and is dependable.

CZ 75

Cold War Wonder Nine
Produced: 1975–Present

Introduced in 1975 at the height of the Cold War, the Czech-manufactured CZ 75 featured traditional all-steel construction, a double-/single-action trigger, hammer-forged barrel and grip holding a double stack of sixteen rounds of 9mm ammunition. The finish on these pistols looks like black epoxy baked on—and it is. It has taken, and is still taking, the United States a while to understand how accurate and affordable these pistols are. They are totally reliable and built like a Soviet tank. Part of the reason the CZ 75 is not as well know as other pistols is because the design was kept top secret by the Soviets, who controlled Czechoslovakia. The Czech armed forces adopted the CZ 75 after the Velvet Revolution in 1989. Numerous militaries and law enforcement agencies around the world use the CZ 75.

Like most semiautomatic pistols of recent design, the CZ 75 uses the Browning lintels locking cam similar to the Browning Hi-Power, and like the SIG P210, the slide of the CZ 75 rides inside the frame rails. This slide and frame configuration aids in the pistol's accuracy.

Jeff Cooper's pet project, the Bren Ten pistol chambered in 10mm, was based on the CZ 75. Many other manufacturers have copied the CZ 75 design and currently produce pistols like EAA in the United States, Sarsilmaz in Turkey, Sphinx in Switzerland, Tanfoglio in Italy, and others.

Right: This traditional all-steel construction CZ 75 is an excellent design offering accuracy and reliability.

Heir Apparent

The EAA Witness Full Size built by Tanfoglio is the heir apparent to the Bren Ten. Jeff Cooper felt the 10mm offered better external ballistics than the .45 ACP, so when the 10mm cartridge debuted in 1983, Norma was the only factory to offer the round and the company of Dornaus & Dixon Enterprises had the only pistol, the Bren Ten. The Bren Ten was based on the CZ 75. TV actor Don Johnson, as Sonny Crocket in *Miami Vice*, used a Bren Ten during a few seasons.

Above: The original Bren Ten, manufactured by Dornaus & Dixon Enterprises, harnessed the power of the 10mm in the CZ 75 platform.

Above: The full-size Witness is the closest pistol currently available that is similar to the Bren Ten.

SIG Sauer P220

America's Introduction to SIG
Produced: 1975–Present

The P220 replaced the SIG P210, which was in use during World War I. The 9mm P210 was renowned for its accuracy due to the design of the slide and frame. The slide rides inside the frame rails, which is the reverse of most semiautomatic pistols. The P220 was designed with a slide and frame set-up in which the slide ran on the outside of the frame. The slide was originally made of stamped sheet steel and the frame was forged alloy. The pistol also operates on the locked breech, short-recoil system designed by John Browning, but instead of the locking lugs milled into the barrel and slide like on a 1911, the P220 locks the barrel and slide together with a breech. Glock uses a similar breechblock lock-up.

Notable features of the P220 include a decocking lever that allows shooters a safe way to lower the hammer. As the decocker lever is depressed, the automatic firing pin lock is engaged. The P220 also has a trigger-activated firing pin block. The double-action/single-action trigger system had been battle tested in the Walther P38, and SIG continued to use this type of system. European models have the magazine latch in the butt. US models have the magazine release aft of the trigger.

The Swiss Army adopted the P220 and designated it the Pistole 75 chambered in 9mm. Many other special forces units adopted the P220 as well, and the 9mm variant evolved into the P226. In the United States the P220 was offered in 9mm, .38 Super, and .45 ACP. That last caliber was the one that caught America's fancy. All current P220s are available only in .45 ACP. Browning Arms imported their branded version of the SIG P220, called the BDA from 1977 through 1980. At the time the pistol was very modern looking, and when most American shooters pictured a .45 ACP pistol, it was the Colt 1911.

I include myself in that once-ignorant bunch. What shooters found when firing the P220 was a very ergonomic, soft-shooting pistol with excellent accuracy. The P220 is also a lot lighter than a full-size 1911, so it is easier to carry. Many law enforcement departments, once enamored with the 9mm

Specifications

CALIBER: .45 ACP

BARREL LENGTH: 4.4 inches

OA LENGTH: 7.7 inches

WEIGHT: 30.4 ounces (unloaded)

STOCK: Black textured polymer

SIGHTS: 3-dot fixed, notch rear/blade front or tritium night sights

ACTION: Short recoil, locked breech, semiautomatic

FINISH: Black hard anodized

CAPACITY: 8+1

round and then the .40 S&W round, have come around to the .45 ACP as a duty cartridge. In 2013 the Connecticut State Police swapped their SIG .40 caliber pistols for the larger .45 ACP P220s. The combination of caliber and pistol ergonomics made the choice for troopers a no-brainer.

Above: The P220 replaced the SIG P210 in 1975; this P210 is a modern version of the pistol used by the Swiss during World War II.

Right: All business, the P220 is one of the most accurate out of the box .45 ACP pistols available.

Navy SEALs Choose MK25

When the Navy SEALs were looking for durable and reliable pistols, they turned to the SIG P226. The MK25 is similar to the P226, but the big difference is the internal components are corrosion-resistant—an important feature when you are a frogman.

Right: The Navy SEALs use a variant of the P226 designated the MK25.

Beretta 680 Series

How the World's Oldest Gunmaker Does an Over-and-Under Production: 1979–Present

The Beretta 680 series of over-and-under shotguns are natural pointers built for hunting or clay target shooting. Beretta's reputation is legendary, with a record of success in international competition. Shooters using Beretta shotguns have won Olympic medals.

The 680 series of over-and-unders was introduced in 1979, first as 682 models built for competitive clay shooting and then as the model 686 and 687 field guns. Beretta over-and-unders offer a quality-built, affordable shotgun that is rugged yet elegant—the amount of luxurious engraving and wood is really unlimited—and designed to be used and fired often. Beretta over-and-unders are excellent examples of quality Italian gunmaking at its best.

To a great extent the 680 series competes head to head with the Browning Citori; the Beretta costs less than the Browning. Go to any trap field or sporting clays course, and you will find most guns are either Berettas or Brownings with their respective users enthusiastic brand ambassadors. Certainly the

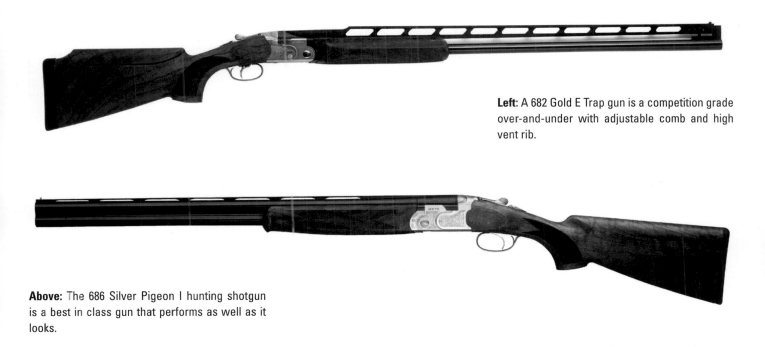

Left: A 682 Gold E Trap gun is a competition grade over-and-under with adjustable comb and high vent rib.

Above: The 686 Silver Pigeon I hunting shotgun is a best in class gun that performs as well as it looks.

Specifications

GAUGE: 12, 20, 28, .410

BARREL LENGTH: 26 to 34 inches

OA LENGTH: 10.75 inches (6-inch barrel), 14.75 inches (10-inch barrel)

WEIGHT: 6.8 pounds (12 gauge, 28-in. barrel)

STOCK: Select checkered walnut (687 Silver Pigeon III)

SIGHTS: Metal bead

RIB TYPE: Flat, .25-in. x .25-in.

ACTION: Low-profile improved boxlock, break action

FINISH: Silvered receiver, matte black barrels, numerous finish options

CAPACITY: 2

Berettas hold an old world status (manufactured in Italy) compared to the Brownings (built in Japan).

The 682 models were built up through 2000 and were known as well-built competition models that featured a trigger with adjustable length of pull, wide top vent ribs, and stocks with palm swells. The 686 and 687 models are still catalogued by Beretta, and over the years they have gone through numerous cosmetic changes. These models are built for upland hunting and offer excellent balance when swinging on a flushing bird. The 687 models are more posh with higher grade figured wood and receivers ornately engraved; 687 Silver Pigeon V and the top of the line 687 EELL Diamond Pigeon models have side plates with gold inlays and rich hand-chased engraving.

What sets the Beretta 680 series apart from other over-and-under shotgun makers in the same price range are the receivers. Beretta receivers are low profile, which is accomplished by placing the lugs halfway up the breechblock

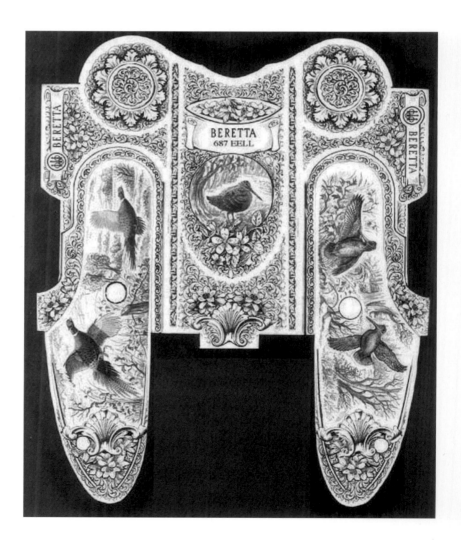

Right: The 687 EELL Classic features hand-chased engraved side plates with intricately detailed motifs.

of the mono bloc constructed barrels, which are copied by a number of other shotgun manufacturers. This set-up creates a slim, compact receiver that is very durable. One 687 EELL Sporting model has documented over 700,000 rounds. Also unique to the Beretta design, the 680 series uses two conical locking lugs located mid-action right between the barrels. This gives the 686 receiver locking strength while keeping the profile lower, allowing the eye of the shooter to be closer to the plane of his or her supporting hand. The pins also self-adjust for wear. The barrels hinge on trunnions set into the receiver sidewalls—another Beretta design detail copied by others. All these details and others, depending on the shotgun's end use, give the 680 series a feel and handling that make them as popular in the field as they are in competition.

Bottom: The author and dog Cooper wait their turn at an informal field trial; that's a Beretta 686 Silver Pigeon II in 20-gauge.

Barrett M82A1

Specifications
CALIBER: .416 Barrett, .50 BMG
BARREL LENGTH: 29 inches
OA LENGTH: 57 inches
WEIGHT: 30.9 pounds (unloaded)
STOCK: Metal
SIGHTS: Adjustable rear/fixed front, optic ready
ACTION: Recoil-operated, semiautomatic
FINISH: Matte black
CAPACITY: 10-round detachable box

Long Range Beast
Produced: 1982–Present

The name Barrett is synonymous with .50 caliber rifles and in particular semiautomatic .50-caliber rifles. For over two decades the M82A1 design has been refined so that it is reliable and accurate in whatever environmental hell it is required to perform. In US Army parlance, the Barrett M82A1 is known as the M107; the USMC designate it as the M82A3. Whatever the name, the rifle harnesses the power of a century-old cartridge in a modern, one-man, portable, shoulder-fired rifle.

The .50 BMG was first introduced in 1910, and it was adopted into military service in 1921 for use in the heavy M2 Browning machine gun. Though other firearms designers have built weapons chambered in .50 BMG, Barrett was able to create a semiautomatic rifle design that was reliable and accurate.

Military agencies around the globe use this light recoiling rifle, which has a maximum effective range of 1,800 meters (1,869 yards). The Swedish Army was the first military organizations to purchase M82A1 rifles. In 1990 the US government employed M82A1s in operations Desert Shield and Desert Storm in Kuwait and Iraq, respectively, using it as an anti-

Below: The Barrett M82A1 is shoulder-fired rifle that fires the .50 BMG cartridge.

Above: A US Marine fires the M107; note the empty cartridge case being ejected. Recoil is very tolerable due to the rifle's design. Courtesy of US Department of Defense.

material weapon able to effectively disable vehicles, parked aircraft, and radar installations among other high-value targets. In the hands of snipers the Barrett can defeat enemy personnel at ranges conventional shoulder weapons can't.

In operation the barrel recoils slightly backward, and then a rotating bolt takes over and spits out the empty cartridge shell and scrapes a fresh round from the magazine. Like the AR platform, the M82A1 has upper and lower receivers. To mitigate recoil the M107 uses a dual-chamber, detachable muzzle brake.

Numerous long-range shots have been made with the M82A1. During the Iraq War in 2004, Sergeant Brian Kremer of the 2nd Ranger Battalion used a Barrett to neutralize enemy targets at a range of 2,515 yards. That's 1.4 miles. In 2008 in Afghanistan, US Army sniper Nicholas Ranstad has a confirmed kill out to 2,288 yards.

Right: At about thirty pounds, including the scope and loaded magazine, the M107 is still very maneuverable and easy to reposition. Courtesy of US Department of Defense.

Right: The .50 BMG (Browning Machine Gun) Mk 211 Mod 0 High-Explosive-Incendiary-Armor-Piercing (HEIAP) cartridge contains a .30-caliber tungsten penetrator, zirconium powder, and Composition A explosive. It can be identified by a green tip with a grey ring.

Desert Eagle

Magnum Powered Brute with Star Quality
Produced: 1982–Present

Robot Cop (the original), *Demolition Man*, *Boondock Saints*, *La Femme Nikita* (the original French version and the Hollywood remake), *The Matrix*, *Year of the Dragon*, *Barb Wire*, *Commando*, *Austin Powers*, *Double Impact*—there are more, a lot more. In fact, the Desert Eagle has appeared in over five hundred movies since the 1980s. It has been used virtually in video games with names like *Counter-Strike*, *Tomb Raider*, *Grand Theft Auto*, and *Call of Duty: Modern Warfare*. TV shows like *Miami Vice*, *The Shield*, *Spenser: For Hire*, *Walker Texas Ranger*, and countless others correctly typecasted the pistol as a menacing blaster with raw power. The Desert Eagle is one of the most iconic and stylistic pistols in all media forms. When Hollywood needs a pistol to wreak havoc and devastation, the Desert Eagle is written into the script.

Below: The classic black Desert Eagle in .50 AE.

Specifications

CALIBER: .357 Magnum, .44 Magnum, .50 Action Express

BARREL LENGTH: 6 or 10 inches

OA LENGTH: 10.75 inches (6-inch barrel), 14.75 inches (10-inch barrel)

WEIGHT: 71.4 ounces

STOCK: Textured rubber

SIGHTS: Fixed rear/ramp front

ACTION: Single-action, semiautomatic

FINISH: Matte black (original), numerous finish options

CAPACITY: 9+1 (.357 Magnum), 8+1 (.44 Magnum), 7+1 (.50 Action Express)

Though the Desert Eagle pistol does have the brutish, if not rakish, good looks of a leading man, it does not just give good face to the camera or splatter opponents into red goo with a flick of a joystick. The Desert Eagle is a serious pistol with fierce firepower that harnesses the power of .50 AE (Action Express) and magnum revolver cartridges in a semiautomatic pistol platform. Loaded with a 300-grain bullet, the .50 AE produces 1476 fps muzzle velocity and 1449 ft-lbs of energy out of a six-inch barrel. The typical .45 ACP with a 230-grain bullet has a 850 fps velocity and produces 369 ft-lbs of energy from a five-inch barrel.

Chambering a pistol in a revolver cartridge is a bit unorthodox and requires extra thought in the engineering of the pistol. Revolver cartridges are rimmed and headspace on the rim, while a typical semiautomatic cartridge like .45 ACP, 9mm, .40 S&W, to name just three, headspace on the case mouth. The rimmed cartridges also pose an engineering problem in the

Left: A .50 AE barrel for a Desert Eagle.

magazine design to ensure the cartridges feed properly. The design of the pistol has numerous patents, with the first awarded to Bernard C. White of Magnum Research, Inc. (MRI) for a gas-actuated pistol. The Desert Eagle uniquely uses a gas-operated mechanism with a rotating bolt, the type of mechanism normally found on rifles like the Ruger Mini-14 and US Military M14.

After initial design and prototypes, MRI contracted Israel Military Industries (IMI) to work out the bugs and refine the design so it could be brought into production. It went through a number of design changes from 1979 through 1982. IMI enhanced the pistol, securing patents along the way, and MRI (along with IMI) initially offered the Desert Eagle in two models: the Mark I and the Mark VII. Both models were available in .357 Magnum and .44 Magnum. The Mark VII had an adjustable trigger and at one time was chambered in .41 Magnum. Later the Mark VII was chambered in .50 Action Express (AE). The current production model is the Mark XIX, an upgrade of the Mark VII. The Mark XIX uses one frame size for all calibers, which allows the operator to change calibers by swapping out barrel, bolt, and magazine. The pistol fieldstrips into six main components.

Left: The Desert Eagle in titanium gold with Bengal tiger stripes for over two thousand dollars.

As in a rifle, the Desert Eagle uses gas from a fired round to articulate the mechanism. Gas is ported from the breech and travels forward through a tube under the barrel, flows into a cylinder, and then pushes the piston rearward. The pistol uses a three-lug rotating bolt with dual recoil springs to bring the slide forward after a shot is fired. This gas system and powerful big-bore magnum calibers bulk up the size of the pistol. Notably, the Desert Eagle is massive. Aside from the rifle-style mechanism, the Desert Eagle uses a barrel locked into the pistol's frame. This allows a higher degree of accuracy. The polygonal rifling is also unique as it reduces barrel wear, is easy to clean, produces a better seal between the bullet and the bore, and aids in accuracy. The chamber is chrome-plated to facilitate easier cartridge case extraction. The grip is designed to help reduce felt recoil and make shooting the powerful rounds easier and more comfortable. The pistol, obviously, was designed to use a two-handed grip. A single-action two-stage trigger system requires the operator to cock the hammer prior to firing the pistol. The Desert Eagle trigger also features ATM (Adjustable Trigger Mechanism) that enables a user to adjust trigger travel between the lighter pull of the first stage to the heavier pull of the second stage. The thumb-operated safety catch is ambidextrous and when in the "ON" position blocks the the firing pin while it disconnects the trigger from the firing mechanism.

As a hunting weapon, the Desert Eagle is quite capable of taking big game. The top of the barrel incorporates a Picatinny-style rail so a low power scope or red dot sight can be attached. If wild pigs are a problem, then a Desert Eagle may be a solution. I have fired a .44 Magnum model with six-inch barrel and found the pistol can quickly convert cement blocks to small chunks and dust.

The finishes offered on the Desert Eagle run the gamut of what one expects from a pistol quite capable of toppling a grizzly bear in real life to co-starring with Sylvester Stallone, Arnold Schwarzenegger, and Pamela Anderson—all-business black matte to a glam 24K gold with tiger stripes. Stainless steel models are offered and have a muzzle brake option.

Though the Desert Eagle has been depicted as a popular combat weapon in mass media, it is impractical in that role. It is heavy (weighing over four pounds), long, and has serious recoil, to name just a few real-world attributes. The Desert Eagle does have an imposing presence and a powerful reputation as a pop culture icon. Not many pistols have been on the cover of *Playboy* magazine in the hands of a pink-bikini-clad Pamela Anderson.

"Coonan" the Barbarian

Not many semiautomatic pistols are chambered in a rimmed revolver cartridge like the Desert Eagle. The Coonan .357 Magnum Automatic is about the only other exception to the rule. The Coonan uses a 1911-style platform but is chambered in .357 Magnum; it also fires .38 Special cartridges when the recoil spring is swapped out. The frame and slide are made of 17-4 PH stainless steel investment castings. The Coonan is an engineering marvel, combining a semiautomatic pistol platform and a rimmed revolver cartridge.

Glock G17

Game Changer
Produced: 1982–Present

Glock did not invent the polymer-framed pistol, but they did create a "plastic pistol" that is durable, reliable, accurate, and changed the way handguns are designed and made. These handguns are ubiquitous and come from a small manufacturer who had no prior knowledge of firearm design. Gaston Glock made small items for the Austrian military from his garage. Glock pistols now have about 65 percent market share among US law enforcement agencies. The 9mm G17 was the first model produced,

Below: Cutaway pistols are used by Glock's sales force to show the inner workings of the weapon; this is one of eight made of a Gen1 Model 17. Courtesy Stanley Ruselowski collection.

and similar models followed in compact and subcompact versions in numerous calibers: .330, 9mm, .40 S&W, 10mm, .357 SIG, .45 ACP, and 45 GAP.

All the pistols operate the same (and in fact look the same). Besides caliber, size is the only other differentiator. Design features include a low slide profile that keeps the barrel axis close to the shooter's hand to reduce muzzle flip, a nylon-based polymer frame with steel inserts, a polygonal rifled barrel, and three independent safety mechanisms: the striker-fire action system, a firing pin safety, and a drop safety. Glock touts perfection, and they come

Below: A Gen1 G17 (top) and a Gen1 G19 (bottom), two of Glock's most popular models with LE. Courtesy Stanley Ruselowski collection.

Specifications

CALIBER: 9mm

BARREL LENGTH: 4.5 inches

OA LENGTH: 7.3 inches

WEIGHT: 22 ounces (unloaded)

STOCK: Textured polymer

SIGHTS: 3-dot fixed, notch rear/ blade front

ACTION: Short recoil, locked breech; striker-fired, semiautomatic

FINISH: Matte black

CAPACITY: 17+1

very close. Disassembly of Glocks is simple, maintenance is minimal, and accuracy is great.

Over the years Glock has revised the grip. There are five texture treatments: Gen1 guns (1986–1988) had a pebble finish, Gen2 guns (1988–1997) had a checkered grenade texture, the Gen3 models (1995–2014) had finger grooves and checkered texture, and the current Gen4 guns (introduced in 2010) have an RTF-4 (Rough Texture Frame), a toned down grip texture from the extreme polymid traction RTF-2 texture, which was considered too aggressive.

The Glock became a heralded "gangster" weapon in rap songs. A slew of rappers from Wu-Tang Clan ("Da Glock") to The Notorious B.I.G. ("Whatchu Want") have glorified the Glock, making more of the population aware of the pistol. TV shows were quick to use the matte black, blocky shaped pistol. *Miami Vice* may have been the first shows to cast the G17 and it just snowballed with *The X-Files*, *The Sopranos*, *CSI: Crime Scene*

Below: Originally Glocks were packed in these Tupperware-like containers. Courtesy Stanley Ruselowski collection.

Investigation, 24, and many more. Mickey Rourke in *Johnny Handsome* was the first actor to wield a G17 in a film in 1989.

Some gun experts snorted and said that no one would ever want a "plastic" gun, it would wear out too soon. The media had a field day assuming the "plastic gun" would get through security metal detectors, when in fact Glocks are 83 percent metal by weight. When the brass cooled and dust settled, Glock dominated law enforcement, was with numerous militaries across the world, and replaced many revolvers and full metal pistols in nightstands.

Heckler & Koch P9

The HK P9 is one of the first successful polymer framed pistols. Produced from 1969 through 1978, it featured a polymer frame with stamp steel reinforcements and polygonal rifling, two design characteristics of the Glock. HK used a roller delayed mechanism and traditional DA trigger. LE or special forces units in countries like Greece, Germany, Japan, Netherlands, and others still use the P9. The Navy SEALS have used a suppressed version of the P9.

Knight MK-85

Specifications	
CALIBER: .50 or .52	
BARREL LENGTH: 26 inches	
OA LENGTH: 45 inches	
WEIGHT: 8.5 pounds	
STOCK: Checkered synthetic	
SIGHTS: Williams adjustable rear/ fiber optic front	
ACTION: Bolt-action, single-shot	
FINISH: Stainless barrel/Realtree camo stock	
CAPACITY: 1	

Inline Blackpowder Pioneer
Production: 1985–2009, 2012–Present

It was a simple idea. Instead of using the traditional side ignition of muzzleloading percussion rifles, Tony Knight created an inline ignition system that completely revolutionized modern muzzleloading rifles. Knight also ditched the centuries-old percussion cap for 209 shot shell primer, and to make it all weatherproof—rain and snow is the bane of traditional muzzle loading rifles—he added the 209 primer to a plastic waterproof disc. Knight also updated the action with a simple bolt system so the rifle looked and worked like a modern bolt-action rifle. This modern design also allowed hunters to mount a scope on the rifle.

The inline design is infinitely more efficient than the traditional sidelock method of ignition, since the cap or primer fires directly into the load of powder instead of igniting the powder from a 90-degree angle. A 209 primer is inserted in a plastic disc, and the disc is then inserted into the rear of the barrel. The plastic disc creates a watertight seal.

Where Tony Knight ventured, all others followed, and today the inline muzzleloader is a preferred choice of hunters across the country.

Above: The Knight MK-85 completely revolutionized muzzleloading rifles with its inline ignition.

Omega's Triumph

The Thompson-Center Omega uses a drop-action system that makes the rifle much shorter and lighter than the bolt-action system used in the Knight MK-85 and similar rifles. The popularity of the drop-action system swung the pendulum away from bolt-action style muzzleloaders to the drop-action. TC refined the Omega—the disc/primer could be difficult to insert with a scope mounted—into the Triumph, which has a break-action that tips the barrel open for ease in loading the disc/primer. The Triumph has only four moving parts and the breech plug can be removed by hand.

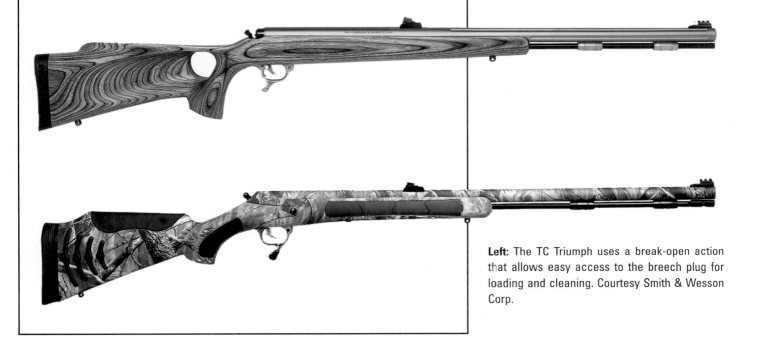

Below: The TC Omega uses the same ignition principle as the Knight muzzleloader but with a different mechanism. Courtesy Smith & Wesson Corp.

Left: The TC Triumph uses a break-open action that allows easy access to the breech plug for loading and cleaning. Courtesy Smith & Wesson Corp.

Krieghoff K-80

Specifications
GAUGE: 12 (3-inch chamber)
BARREL LENGTH: 30 or 32 inches
WEIGHT: 8.75 lbs.
STOCK: Turkish walnut
FRONT SIGHT: White bead front, metal center bead
ACTION: Break action
FINISH: Blued
CAPACITY: 2

The Model 32 Reborn
Produced: 1988–Present

The Remington Model 32 was introduced during the Great Depression in 1931 when the norm in shotguns included pumps, side-by-sides, single-shots, and semiautomatics. The American shooting public was not ready for an over-and-under shotgun. That would happen with the Browning Superposed at around the same time. The fact was the Remington Model 32 was a well-built shotgun. A bit over five thousand of the standard models were built, much less for target models. All was dust for the Model 32 until 1986 when H. Krieghoff in Ulm, Germany, was founded. The firm resurrected the Model 32 as the K-80, and competition shooters have yet again forgotten the Model 32 because they are too busy shooting their K-80s.

Below: The Krieghoff K-80 Pro Sporter is a very popular gun for sporting clay competition.

Benelli Super Black Eagle II

A 3-1/2 Inch That Is Simple, Simple, Simple
Production: 1991–Present

If my high school physics teacher had used a Benelli semiautomatic shotgun to demonstrate the concept of inertia, I would have paid closer attention. Most Benelli semiautomatic shotguns—particularly the M2 and the SBE (Super Black Eagle) II—use an operating system developed in 1967 that is extremely simple. With just three main parts—bolt body, inertia spring, rotating bolt head—the SBE II and M2 can just about run forever without cleaning. Outfitters in Central America and South America use Benelli for one main reason: they run forever. Well, maybe two reasons: Shooters can hit doves and other flying beasties with these clean running and fast handling shotguns.

Below: As sure as the sun rises, so will the SBE II keep working no matter what the hunting conditions; numerous finish choices and stock configurations are offered.

Specifications

GAUGE: 12 (2-3/4 in., 3 in., 3-1/2 in.)

BARREL LENGTH: 24 to 28 inches

OA LENGTH: 45.6 inches (24-inch barrel) to 49.6 inches (28-inch barrel)

WEIGHT: 7.1 pounds (24-inch barrel) to 7.3 pounds (28-inch barrel)

STOCK: Satin walnut, black synthetic, or Realtree camo

SIGHTS: Red bar front, metal bead mid rib

ACTION: Inertia-operated, semiautomatic

FINISH: Matte black or Realtree camo

CAPACITY: 3+1

Inertia is the tendency for an object at rest to remain at rest, so when a round is fired the Benelli moves rearward while the bolt body stays in position due to the inertia spring—a short, thick spring inside the bolt body. Nearly the entire shotgun is a recoiling component; only the bolt remains stationary during firing. Benelli's inertia-driven system is often compared to gas-operated systems like those found in Mossberg 930 and 935, Remington 1100 and 11-87, Browning Gold, and other semiautomatic shotguns. Gas-operated systems divert burning gases from fired shells to a piston system that operates the mechanism. Burning powder and gas—all that soot and gunk—is contained in the barrel of the Benelli so the action stays cleaner and cooler than a gas-operated action. The SBE II and M2 also use fewer moving parts than gas-operated shotguns. The end result is slightly more felt recoil with the inertia driven system compared to gas-operated systems, but the shotgun stays cleaner and cooler and is much more reliable. When other semiautos stop running, the SBE II keeps going and going.

Waterfowl hunters in ducks blinds or boats and goose hunters hunkered down in frozen fields have come to rely on the SBE II. When temperatures are below freezing and your breath freezes to your beard, other semiautos can refuse to work, but the SBE II chugs along with a reliability that hunters come to take for granted. Another appealing aspect of the SBE II is its handling characteristics. Unlike some 3-1/2-inch chambered semiautos that handle like a piece of 2x4 lumber, the SBE II handles like an over-and-under. It is well-balanced and responsive. As a turkey hunting shotgun the SBE II can be set up with Benelli's SteadyGrip, which is just a fancy name for a pistol grip stock. Sitting with your back to tree, the pistol grip stock makes shooting more comfortable. Deer hunters who use slug guns can also get the SBE II set up for whitetails with a 24-inch rifle barrel. The SBE II is a machine that is reliable and hard working. Some critics might say the SBE II is too light to shoot 3-1/2-inch shells comfortably. In my opinion the only time shooting 3-1/2-inch shells is comfortable is when your hunting partner is pulling the trigger.

Left: Got Ducks? The SBE II with 3-1/2-in. chambers has what it takes to bring high flyers down.

No Inertia, But USMC Approved

The USMC calls the Benelli M4 the M1014. In 1988 when the Marines were shopping around for a new combat shotgun they chose the M4 after extensive testing at the Aberdeen Proving Grounds. The M4 crushed the competition. The M4 uses Benelli's Auto-Regulating Gas-Operated (A.R.G.O.) system. This system, like all Benelli systems, is simple. Two stainless-steel self-cleaning pistons located just forward of the chamber, where burning gases are hotter and cleaner, push directly against the bolt. There are no action rods like typical gas-piston-operated shotguns.

Beretta AL391

Specifications
GAUGE: 20 or 12
BARREL LENGTH: 24, 26, 28, 30, and 32 inches
OA LENGTH: 51 inches (28-in. barrel)
WEIGHT: 7.3 pounds (28-in. barrel, 12-gauge)
STOCK: Glossy walnut or synthetic
SIGHTS: Bead or fiber optic front, bead mid rib
ACTION: Gas-operated, semiautomatic
FINISH: Blued or silver receiver/ blued barrel
CAPACITY: 3+1

Reliable with Less Kick
Production: 1999–2013

Semiautomatic shotguns in 12-gauge have a dual role. First, they shouldn't be too heavy to carry, because hunters may need to walk a lot while toting pounds of steel and stock. Second, the recoil should not loosen the fillings in your teeth. The AL390 series of shotguns have always been great performers. The AL391 series were even better due to a self-compensating gas valve and a receiver recoil absorber making the gun reliable to shoot without a bruised shoulder.

I have an AL391 Xtreme2 that I have used for turkey hunting. We all remember touching off our first 3-1/2-inch turkey load. For some, that was enough to stick with 2-3/4-inch loads and learn to better call in a wily tom. The shotgun is fairly light—7.8 pounds—for such a heavy hitter, and it also has a KO (Kick Off) recoil reduction that is not anything new, but it works. The Xtreme has been used for fowl in the coldest of duck blinds. With certain loads on coyote it is deadly.

Below: The Teknys model of the AL391 followed the Ulrika model; this Teknys has a sculpted receiver and is designed for sporting clays.

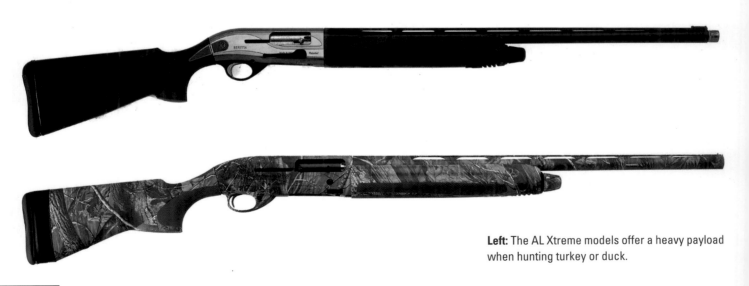

Left: The AL Xtreme models offer a heavy payload when hunting turkey or duck.